WE DO

ALSO BY STAN TATKIN, PSYD, MFT

Books

Wired for Dating:
How Understanding Neurobiology and Attachment
Style Can Help You Find Your Ideal Mate

Wired for Love:
How Understanding Your Partner's Brain and
Attachment Style Can Help You Defuse Conflict
and Build a Secure Relationship

Love and War in Intimate Relationships:
Connection, Disconnection, and
Mutual Regulation in Couple Therapy
(coauthored with Marion Solomon)

Audio Programs

Relationship Rx: Insights and Practices to
Overcome Chronic Fighting and Return to Love

Your Brain on Love:
The Neurobiology of Healthy Relationships

WE DO

SAYING YES
TO A
RELATIONSHIP
OF DEPTH, TRUE
CONNECTION,
AND ENDURING
LOVE

STAN TATKIN

PSYD, MFT

sounds true
BOULDER, COLORADO

Sounds True
Boulder, CO 80306

Published 2018

Cover design by Jennifer Miles
Book design by Beth Skelley

Printed in Canada

Library of Congress Cataloging-in-Publication Data

Names: Tatkin, Stan, author.
Title: We do : saying yes to a relationship of depth, true connection,
   and enduring love / Stan Tatkin, PsyD, MFT.
Description: Boulder, Colorado : Sounds True, 2018. |
   Includes bibliographical references.
Identifiers: LCCN 2018014052 (print) | LCCN 2018015336 (ebook) |
   ISBN 9781622038947 (ebook) | ISBN 9781622038930 (pbk.)
Subjects: LCSH: Marriage–Psychological aspects | Couples–Psychology. |
   Intimacy (Psychology) | Interpersonal relations. | Interpersonal conflict.
Classification: LCC HQ728 (ebook) | LCC HQ728 .T248 2018 (print) |
   DDC 306.81–dc23
LC record available at https://lccn.loc.gov/2018014052

10 9 8 7 6 5 4 3 2 1

This book is dedicated to my wife, Tracey Boldemann-Tatkin,
to whom I owe my freedom, my safety, my security, and the resources
with which I could write this book. And to my stepdaughter,
Joanna, who would fight every battle for me, if I wished.
Thank you, my loves, for putting up with your pain in the ass.

CONTENTS

INTRODUCTION

WHY SHOULD YOU "WE DO?"

As a couple therapist, I'm constantly seeing partners who have made many mistakes right from the very beginning. I know that if I had seen them before marriage, I could have predicted the troubles they would later share with me. This may sound arrogant and presumptuous, but once you understand what works and what can never work in any love relationship, you come to understand the trajectory of failed marriages. I wish I had known this many years ago when my first marriage ended and before I'd learned the skills and attitude necessary for a healthy, secure-functioning relationship, which I'm living today with my wife, Tracey. I'm writing this book now because I believe in prevention. If I know that when marriages start improperly they also run aground predictably, why not send out a clarion call to those just beginning their commitment journey?

I've witnessed many individuals engage in major endeavors without first learning about them. For instance, many people who want to become parents will avoid or refuse to seek counsel, support, or even books and articles that would help prepare them for the road ahead. Many folks who are becoming stepparents jump right in without the benefit of reading literature or getting counseling that can help prepare them for stepparenting. Major life endeavors such as marriage, stepparenting, or parenting require preparation. Perhaps individuals ignore counsel because people, generally speaking, don't like being told what to do. Many people think that marriage, like child-rearing or stepparenting, should come naturally, as if we're born with a road map on how to do it well. Because of the business I'm in, I see clearly that very few people have that road map.

What I'm saying here should interest *both* you and your partner, not just one of you. If only one of you is interested in learning what I have to say to you in this book, that right there may be a huge problem. If ignored, I may see you in my office sooner rather than later.

I don't want to use a stick when there really is a carrot here. There are huge benefits to partnering, which I will say a lot about throughout this book. My purpose here isn't to put the fear of God into you but rather to help you save yourself time and grief by not reinventing the wheel. If reading this book can make both of you happier, healthier, more successful, and better people, would that be worth your while?

I intend to give you all that I currently know and understand about love relationships, particularly committed love relationships. You will come to see that learning to become secure-functioning partners is a process of *we do* and not *I do*—which is why I want you to read this book together and follow the many exercises and suggestions it lays out. Like marriage, reading this book is a two-person endeavor, not a one-person project. And that, my friends, is the big message in this written work. "We do" means just that. We either do this together, as a team, or we don't do this at all.

One more thing. I, along with many of my heroes in the field of relationships—Harville Hendrix and Helen LaKelly Hunt, Marion Solomon, Ellyn Bader and Peter Pearson, John and Julie Gottman, Daniel J. Siegel, and Sue Johnson—agree with the basic principles of secure functioning as laid out in this book.[*] Though we each have our various approaches, we agree that our culture has shifted too far in the direction of *me-ism* and away from *we-ism*.

WHY "WE DO?"

Before I continue, dear friends, I want to address my fear that you may be misled by the mixed cultural messages about *pair-bonding*—a fancy term

---

[*] Relationships First, a nonprofit organization committed to cultivating healthy relationship skills in couples, families, communities, and institutions, was founded by Harville Hendrix and Helen LaKelly Hunt. Other founding members include the above, me, and my wife, Tracey Boldemann-Tatkin.

for "hooking up." Not only is happiness a result of secure relationships but it's also a predictor of longevity and physical health. Let me begin by citing a seventy-nine-year (as of this writing) longitudinal study of men and happiness. It began with the Grant Study at Harvard Medical School in 1938 and has since branched out into other studies to become the longest running human study ever.[1] Dr. George Vaillant, who directed the study for more than thirty years, and Dr. Robert Waldinger, who directs the project today, conclude that "warmth of relationships throughout life has the greatest positive impact on 'life satisfaction.'" Vaillant states this more succinctly in his assessment of the study: "Happiness is love. Full stop."[2]

AN OUNCE OF PREVENTION

Still, approximately 42 percent of first marriages end in divorce, and the average length of those marriages is only eight years. Sixty percent of second marriages end in divorce. Seventy-three percent of all third marriages end in divorce. If you want to beat the odds, what's the best way? Prevention! Prevention by becoming experts on each other, accepting each other "as is," becoming excellent co-managers of each other's nervous system, creating unassailable shared principles of purpose and vision, managing thirds properly, and engaging in a secure-functioning manner that's collaborative, fair, just, and sensitive.

What I offer in this book is a psychobiological approach to couple work, which simply means that I consider both psychological and biological factors as to how we connect and relate to one another. Psychologically, I focus heavily on family history and on our early experiences of how we bonded with others—our parents and siblings, for example. Biologically, I focus on how our brain, arousal system, and physical health influence our approach to relationships. This includes how you "read" your partner, as well as how you manage each other on an emotional and energetic level. Research tells us that both our psychology and biology are major factors for predicting long-term relationship success. Luckily most of these factors are malleable and subject to change. Relationships affect and change our biology for better or worse.

There's a lot of advice out there for couples planning to tie the knot, to move in together, to have a family together—to "commit." You can get help from books, talk shows, counselors, workshops, and friends. Unfortunately much of this advice, though helpful at times, lacks psychological depth, comprehensiveness, and a research-based, systematic approach. Clergy who offer premarital counseling often use interviews— or a questionnaire-oriented process—that fail to prepare couples for the long journey ahead. Premarital counseling within a secular context suffers from the same problems. I'm not suggesting you avoid meeting with a member of your clergy to get spiritual advice prior to marrying, but rather that you use this book alongside the spiritual guidance you receive. This book takes a science-and-research-based approach to the matter of human pair-bonding that includes developmental neuroscience, arousal regulation, and attachment theory, all in plainspoken language.

A primary purpose of this book is *early prevention*, and the preemptive methods discussed throughout are based on my Psychobiological Approach to Couple Therapy (PACT), developed out of both infant and adult attachment research, marital outcome studies, and developmental neurobiological capacity models (what people are able to do on a social-emotional level). We will spend a few chapters discussing the psychology of relationships, because your past experiences relating with others, especially those from childhood, impact you today. I aim to help you prevent future marital problems rather than sit back and wait to help you solve those problems after they occur. Although therapy can be very valuable down the line, there's a greater risk that it will come too late when you haven't addressed core needs, desires, styles of relating, and mutually agreed-upon principles of power and direction. Together, let's set up your relationship from the get-go so that it has all the elements it needs to succeed.

So I start off this book with a strong message to you: no matter where you stand on marriage or commitment, your relationships and their quality will greatly influence (if not determine) your health and happiness in life. That's because you need other people for a whole lot of important things, only one of which is companionship. Adult human beings require at least one other adult human being (not a child) to help with self-esteem, self-knowledge, self-discovery, and self-improvement. You need another person for silly things, such as letting you know if you have spinach in your teeth, and more significant things, such as helping you understand what you don't know (and there are tons of things you don't know). You need another person to trust. (I bet you thought I would say that you need another person to trust you. That's true as well, and it's certainly nice. But the first is, well, first.) You *need* to love and you *need* to trust. And that's where secure-functioning relationships come in. More on that soon.

Although I believe in committed relationships (whether marriage or partnership) and have dedicated my life's work to helping couples have healthy, sustainable, and enjoyable connections, it's clear that the state of marriage is currently in flux. Will marriage continue as an institution in the United States? Or in the West in general? Or even in the world? As of this writing, Japanese young people aren't getting married. They're not even having sex. Millennials may be changing the rules, though it's too early to tell. New sexual freedoms are attracting subcultural movements to change the definition of love relationships from monogamy to polyamory. If so, offering a new "premarital handbook" may be as relevant to some as selling buggy whips. Yet I don't believe pair-bonding will cease to exist because pair-bonding and mating aren't culturally determined practices. Rather, they're biological drives hardwired into the human species. Therefore, this book has enormous relevance (phew) regardless of whether you're using the *m* word (*marriage*) or the *c* word (*commitment*). I think it's safe to say that committed love relationships will never go out of style.

So let me also start with a promise. I wrote this book because I want you to have a successful relationship. My promise is that if you and your prospective partner adopt the principles and skills I describe here, your relationship *will* be successful—not just for starters but for the long run. This may sound like a grandiose promise, but because this book offers a unique and comprehensive kind of premarital or precommitment counseling, it helps you and your partner look seriously at important questions and considerations as you form your "We Do" relationship. Trust me, it's possible!

Sure, executing the plan put forth in this book may seem challenging at first, but that's because we're talking about two people here, not just one—two different brains, different needs, different histories, different desires, and different personalities. As a couple therapist, I'm often approached with questions from individuals. I can never properly answer those questions because I need to see both partners in action. There's no way to understand a couple system without studying both partners' moment-by-moment interactions. And it's not the therapist who actually needs to understand the partners. The partners need to understand each other deeply and accurately. That can only be accomplished by a thorough partner-partner investigation, deliberation, and accord. To do that, however, takes knowing what to investigate and deliberate, and how to create agreement without compromise.

WHY I WROTE THIS BOOK

Until *We Do*, I wrote mostly about the psychobiology of couples and about secure functioning. In my books *Wired for Love* and *Wired for Dating*, I delve into attachment styles, brain function, relationship improvement, and appropriate mate identification, which we will touch on here too. But *We Do* is different. It's intended to prepare you and your partner for marriage, in all its incarnations, so that you can set your relationship on the right path from the very beginning. It's my most comprehensive work to date. This book isn't simply about deciding if your partner is right or wrong for you. Rather, it prepares you and your partner for the long road ahead and provides you with the best possible launch, tools, and attitude for now and for the future.

Current models of premarital guidance offer little in the way of helping partners know each other as well as what they will be fighting about for the next twenty years. These models also do little to frame marriage in terms of secure functioning. In this book I aim to provide you with a vision of partnership that will be complex enough to help you and your partner through even the worst problems known to arise in marriage as well as prepare you for the good to come. Secure functioning means that you and your partner can operate as a two-person psychological system as fully collaborative, cooperative, and mutually protective.

HOW TO USE THIS BOOK

In the first two chapters, we cover the secrets to a successful marriage. Next, we look at the issues that affect couples most, including the negative brain; the troublesome triad of memory, perception, and communication; and attachment styles. Finally, we will examine how well you know each other, which includes a lengthy discussion on how to identify and deal with any deal breakers that could threaten your relationship. Later, I also include in-depth discussions on sex and how to fight well.

Most self-help books address one person, and that's sufficient if the only subject of the book is you. However, in two-person psychological systems, *both* individuals need to understand and accept the same principles or complications will arise. One person is complicated enough but a two-person system is ever more complex.

Most partners won't read a book together and that's partly because self-help books for couples are often aimed at one person, and one person can't get a relationship into its most alive and healthy state. It's the proverbial sound of one hand clapping. Very hard to hear. If you want to create a successful marriage, you need to be on the same page together, reading with all four eyes, listening with all four ears, and engaging with your two hearts.

For this reason I wrote this book to be read by both partners. If you read it by yourself, and even if you completely buy into the ideas it contains, that will do little good unless your partner does as well. Instead, read it to each other in real time or simply make certain you both read each chapter and then discuss it together. Finally, *We Do* is for all committed relationships whether for marriage or something else. *We Do* is about we-ism or *we-dom*—not me, not I. We're moving into a new era of interdependence, of *we-ness*, and away from social idealization of independence and supercilious labeling of codependence. I hope to convince you as to why this is true. I intend to show you how the human condition is universal, how interdependency isn't merely preferential. Rather, it's a part of our biology and genetic heritage. As you read you will come to understand that we require at least one other person upon whom we can depend, trust, and be tethered to in order to live longer and healthier.

I want to again urge you to read this book together. You might trade off reading each chapter to each other and then talking about it. Try to be understanding of each other's thoughts and opinions about the book's material. It's possible, even likely, that one of you will react strongly to some ideas. Don't worry about that. Just let these concepts float a bit in your head. They make more sense as you continue through the book. Each chapter contains concepts, explanations, examples, and exercises. Some of the experiments, exercises, and games presented in the book may be more useful than others, depending upon your particular interests and needs. Be sure to do them together.

For those of you who are science nerds, the ideas presented here aren't simply personal opinion. They're grounded in research from infant and adult attachment, neuroscience, developmental psychology, strategic and structural systems theory, object relations theory, affect and arousal regulation theory, marital outcome studies, facial expression and body language models, and well-known human stress models. Rather than get into the weeds with the backend of this material, I've spared you the technicalities, for the most part, and focused on what to seek, avoid, and understand in your foray into we-dom. You can read from cover to cover, or you can concentrate on chapters that call out to you.

I present a lot of information to help you get to know each other better. Some of this is deep psychological stuff and comes with a caution: This material should never be used to diagnose yourself or your partner, nor should it be used to demean, dismiss, or attack yourself or your partner. Scientists and researchers study large populations to understand norms and behaviors. While their research gives us a bird's-eye view, individuals are unique, and their behavior should be interpreted by someone who can bridge the gap between the scientific categorizations presented in this book and the behavior of real individuals. So tread lightly and don't pigeonhole. Consult with an expert instead.

I like to teach by using case examples. Please keep in mind that these examples are composites of real cases and don't represent any real individual or couple. I've seen so many couples over so many years that it's impossible to know how "made up" these people are; therefore any likeness to persons living or dead is purely coincidental or at least unintended.

I've also filled the book with many exercises, some of which involve making sustained eye contact while abstaining from talking. While this is important, I realize several people will complain. Holding eye contact with your partner may feel uncomfortable at first, but it's so important, which you will understand better once you work with the material.

Okay? Now let's get started on *We Do*.

1

THE SECRET TO A
SUCCESSFUL MARRIAGE

As I wait at the altar for my radiant bride, Tracey, I ponder our love, the richness of this moment, and the long journey that got me to this point. Tracey, the statuesque blonde I first met in junior high school science class and crushed on (through high school), was about to commit to sharing her life with me. Around the time I was reintroduced to Tracey, I was still a member of the walking wounded. My first marriage had ended in divorce, triggering all kinds of questions and self-doubt. I kept asking myself, Why did this happen to me? Was it me? Was it her? Did we start out with enough in common? Did we grow apart? If we had done something differently, would our marriage have survived? And if so, what? The "us" question never occurred to me, even though how we functioned as a couple was more important than anything we did or didn't do as individuals. As Tracey nears the altar and I get ready to say "I do" for a second time, I know this time it's different—very different—because this time instead of "I do" both of us are saying "We do."

WE DO IS DIFFERENT FROM I DO

I've spent years discovering what makes marriage work, and I will share what I've learned with you in this book so your marriage starts on solid ground. After working with couples for decades, I know that when faced with conflict, differing priorities, and communication problems, you need to have the skills to repair or strengthen your bond. This isn't a book on "you do" or "I do" but rather an opportunity for both partners to focus on "we do." *We* become experts on each other and *we* know just how to handle each other without using fear, threat, or guilt. *We* use attraction to get what we want, prevent what we don't want, and create win-win results. *We* take care of business quickly and efficiently in a manner that's good for both of us. *We* move together happily or we don't move until we make it such.

All successful long-term relationships are what I call *secure-functioning* relationships. They're reliable, dependable, trustworthy, reciprocal, and most definitely respectful. Through secure functioning we form healthy attachments with one another. You and your partner take care of each other in ways that ensure that you both feel safe, secure, protected, accepted, and loved at all times. Secure functioning can be observed all over the world, across socioeconomic strata, and among those with varying physical and mental health issues. It's a set of principles and decisions between two individuals based on survival and begins with the idea that we have each other's back. Only secure-functioning relationships predict well-being and contentment because they operate according to principles of fairness, justice, and sensitivity.

Let me quickly define these terms as We Do concepts. *Fairness* is experienced in partnerships where there's balance, mutuality, and equality. Unfairness might be that I indulged in something at your cost. *Justice* is recompense for that behavior. I make amends, repair, or right the wrong. *Sensitivity* is my awareness of and care for you and your sensibilities, vulnerabilities, and experience of me. In other words, sensitivity refers to my holding you in mind as I speak and act.

All couples, if together long enough, will suffer the vicissitudes of life's fortunes and misfortunes. Even the most solid couple will be tested over time with unforeseen losses, challenges, and frustrations. Think of it this way: the mark of a good couple is how much load bearing the partnership can take without crumbling. In my experience, what determines the success or failure of a romantic relationship isn't common issues such as money, time, messiness, sex, or kids, nor is it about common interests, personality, or differences in age. In other words, it isn't the content of the stressors that causes a relationship to crumble but how we engage with those stressors as a couple. How we work with each other, listen to each other, and calm each other is what matters most.

A secure-functioning relationship:

- provides safety and security

- requires co-management (a.k.a. coregulation) of emotional states

- is collaborative and cooperative

- means accepting each other "as is"

- includes proper management of thirds

- sets the stage for personal growth and well-being

- exists due to shared principles of purpose and vision

Safety and Security

Beyond happiness, beyond joy, beyond sharing good times and bad, the main purpose for pair-bonding (other than procreation) is survival—the need to feel safe and secure in the world. We have a mutual need to survive in an unpredictable world. I realize this may sound alarmist, but it's also reality. Your environment contains predators, which, though unlikely to kill you, pose outside threats.

A couple represents the smallest unit of a society. The two of you are a survival team. Like patrol car partners, your lives depend on each other. You're on the beat together. You protect each other *from* each other and from everyone and everything else. If partners don't understand that their principal function is to keep each other safe from each other and from the outside world, they will trivialize the meaning of their partnership and lessen the likelihood of creating a strong, interdependent relationship.

THREAT

It's important at this juncture to differentiate between big *T* and small *t* threats. Exposure to violence, life threat, or physical abuse of any kind, including sexual, is of the big *T* kind. If you experience any big *T* threat in your current relationship, GET OUT NOW! Seek help immediately and forget about this book until you're safe.

If you have been a victim of physical or sexual abuse or life threat, your partner must be informed and must be deemed an appropriate healing partner for you. More on this important topic later.

Small *t* threat is what we all experience with strangers and nonstrangers alike. It could be your partner turning away from you as you talk about important matters, or it could be the tone of your voice that reminds your partner of dismissiveness or derision. In other words, small *t* threat can be perceived through the face, eyes, body, voice, touch, words, and phrases, all without any malicious intent.

Co-management of Emotional States

Imagine you and your partner are standing on a flat board without guardrails in the middle of some large body of water. As waves roll in and the breeze blows, the two of you must balance this board or you will both fall over. It's definitely hard work to do on a daily basis, yet you have little choice. Where one goes, so goes the other. This, in essence, is co-management of emotional states (a.k.a. coregulation).

A couple's ability to operate as a coregulatory team determines the success or failure of that relationship and is fundamental to relationship safety, security, and longevity. You're now a two-person system with interdependent nervous systems, wiring together like entangled ivy. These two nervous systems represent coregulatory team members that depend on each other for co-managing all emotional states.

One of the concerns when coregulating states is how quickly and effectively each partner co-manages distress and circumvents sustained experiences of threat. A couple who repeatedly induces too much perceived threat will eventually alter each other's biology to become increasingly sensitive to cues *perceived* as menacing. This will eventually increase the rate of errors when appraising each other's thoughts, feelings, and intentions.

Tracey and I have become competent caregivers and handlers of each other. Wow—that sounds bad, as if we're animal handlers or business managers. Okay, consider this: As soon as we understand a child's internal struggle, we can be more loving and exacting with our own behavior. Feeling as if we're experts in what we do and who we do it with makes us happier, more attuned, and more loving. In contrast, without proper coregulation, we may feel persecuted, angry, anxious, and distancing.

As a couple therapist, I find coregulation somewhat mystifying. It's nearly impossible to predict which couples will be good at it, and many couples seem to struggle. Yet I've witnessed great coregulators, young and old, sane and insane, new to marriage and veterans of marriage. The good news is that the two of you, if good coregulators, can repair and correct old, unresolved fears and concerns more quickly and effectively than any therapist can do.

Collaboration and Cooperation

Remember in preschool when you were taught how to cooperate and collaborate with other children? As you will come to understand, secure-functioning partners operate in that fashion as adults. They behave in a truly mutual fashion. You will be a team, having each other's back—cooperative and collaborative. You can think of your secure-functioning relationship as a ship that allows partners to travel together to all corners of the inner and outer world, through place and time, as representatives of what's possible when people work well and play well together. The general spirit of cooperation and collaboration infuses a secure-functioning relationship with trust and dispenses of the need to track every deed. If a partner has a difficult time trusting anyone, perhaps a secure-functioning relationship isn't for them. The same goes for the person who believes it's good to be king or queen; that is, someone who is reluctant to share the load.

Most often these noncollaborative relationships are relics of older models whereby partners witnessed this kind of inequity. In some earlier American models of marriage, divisions of labor were clearly drawn by traditional lines: the husband went to work, and the wife took care of the household, including everyone in it. Few people voiced complaints because everyone seemed on board. Things have changed in many ways. Traditional notions will likely be rejected by at least one partner.

One of the greatest hallmarks of secure functioning is collaboration. Partners who don't collaborate often live separate lives, engage in a dictatorship, or live codependently. Will you collaborate on finances? Housework? Planning vacations? Collaboration doesn't mean that you do everything jointly. It means that you make decisions collectively, even the ones where you decide which ones you must make together.

Acceptance of Each Other As Is

If we did an autopsy on all failed relationships, the number of couples where at least one of the partners was ambivalent—either not all in or waiting for their partner to change—would be very high. There's nothing more pernicious to the safety and security of a primary romantic relationship than a closeted ambivalent partner. If you don't or can't accept your partner as they are right now, without cherry-picking the parts you like, you're in trouble already. Nobody signs up for marriage because they want to be changed by their partner. It doesn't work. Ever. Go all in or go home. Marriage and commitment can only work if we accept each other wholeheartedly.

We live in a culture where no choice is permanent. There's always more than one option. We remain on the fence. It feeds a fantasy of perfection. If we just hold out long enough, that more perfect [fill in the blank] will appear. There *is* no perfect! There's no ideal partner either. There's only the *good enough* partner who is perfectly imperfect. If your partner is willing to do secure functioning with you—and I mean, they're really on board—then that partner *is* perfect for *you*! But you both must take each other as is or not at all. All people are difficult and annoying—that includes you! No matter what it is you don't like about your partner, remember that you're no picnic either.

Proper Management of Thirds

A *third* is anything, anyone, or any activity that's other than the two of you. Thirds can be people, pets, or things, including work, hobbies, or substances. Proper management of thirds means partners protect each other from family members, friends, ex-partners, and so forth, and don't let other activities threaten their safety and security. Both partners are good stewards of what we will call their *couple bubble* (stay tuned). Secure-functioning partners jealously guard their resources and their primary relationship (primacy) from outside bids for attention or competing elements that would threaten one or the other partner. Mismanagement includes throwing your partner under a bus and failing to protect them from thirds. This happens all too often as the following example demonstrates.

Martha and David, both in their midtwenties, were to be married in three months. David, an African American, met Martha, a young woman of German descent, at a community theater production. Martha's father, a domineering figure, openly disapproved of David because of his career choice: a working television actor. Her father's disdain for David also appeared to be race related. The father, a wealthy, deeply conservative businessperson, wanted Martha to marry someone with a better pedigree (read: white, and not an actor). Martha's mother was silent on this matter, which, to David, meant she endorsed her husband's sentiments. Instead of protecting David from her parents, Martha put him in harm's way by asking him to "make nice" with her father. Despite the fact that David was becoming increasingly uncomfortable in her father's presence, Martha kept insisting that David try to make things right with Dad. She defended her father's rude behavior by saying, "I've always been his little princess. He's just trying to protect me." Martha seemed blind to her father's feelings about her black fiancé. She believed that her father wanted stability for her, something an actor couldn't provide. But David knew when he was being judged for his race.

Martha never understood that she was mismanaging thirds right from the start, sacrificing David to please her father. Mismanaging thirds injures at least one partner, but chronic mismanagement often destroys the relationship. It's experienced as a betrayal of the couple's primacy, but it's also tantamount to a deal breaker if one partner fails to see it as a problem.

Setting the Stage for Personal Growth and Well-Being

When your relationship exhibits consistently high levels of secure functioning, you and your partner automatically increase the resources you're able to use for personal development, mutual physical and mental health, and protection from each other and the outside world. You become more resilient as individuals and as a couple, able to manage the slings and arrows of life and its unknowns. You become better people, parents, neighbors, and citizens. Your creativity and productivity are likely to advance along with a greater sense of fearlessness to deal with your particular dragons. This may begin to sound like snake oil, and that I'm prescribing secure functioning for all that ails you—even baldness, old age, poverty, and so forth. I consider myself secure functioning, yet I'm still bald and my aging face continues to melt before me every morning I look in the mirror. No, it's not snake oil, and it's not a unicorn either.

Your personal growth depends on your relationship remaining safe and secure at all times, because if either of you feel the least bit unsafe, untrusting, or insecure, you won't have the internal resources for personal growth. Instead, your mind and body will be preoccupied by doubt and threat. Without a secure-functioning relationship, your creativity, work efficiency, likability, strength, and courage to slay dragons will be greatly compromised. Further, your physical health depends on secure functioning with your partner. Being alone and not having someone upon whom to depend and trust (with your life) is very bad for your health. But so is being in a threat-filled, insecure love relationship.

Shared Principles of Purpose and Vision

Secure-functioning partners are equals and held to mutually agreed-upon principles of governance. Without a common purpose that serves *both* partners, the default will be . . . what? How are the two of you going to govern—each other and everyone else? How are you going to protect yourselves from each other and from those outside your partnership?

Priorities

Before I go any further, let me speak to the question of priorities in the secure-functioning world. We all operate according to priorities from highest to lowest. But I'm not referring to tasks or organizational management. I'm asking you to think about and answer these questions: What's your highest priority going forward? Where are you pointing? What's your vision for yourself and your partner? For instance, is your highest priority your work or career? Is it your children (if you have any)? Is it to have a family of your own? Is it self-development, freedom, or other self-interests? Or is your highest priority your relationship, your partner? Clarity—yours and your partner's—is vital to your happiness and your partnership.

Secure functioning doesn't mean that your relationship with your partner must come first, but it *does* mean that you must know what your highest priority *is* so you don't set yourself up for big problems. (I believe, personally, that relationships do best when they come first.) Both you *and* your partner must be clear on priorities and you must agree, otherwise there *will* be trouble. Your highest priority will predict the decisions you both make down the line. However, it's critical that the two of you absolutely agree on this matter and be able to argue why and how it serves both a personal and a mutual good. In other words, why is this a good idea for "me *and* you?" If you can't clarify your highest priority, mutually agree, and be able to explain why it's a good priority for you and your partner, then you're *not* secure functioning. Make sense?

I suggest that your highest priority should be the relationship. As secure-functioning partners who put the relationship first, you elevate yourselves to a higher purpose. You serve the relationship and the relationship provides you both with safety, security, and absolute trust, from which you both benefit. When you take fears, doubts, distrust, and insecurities off the table, you can be there to comfort, soothe, excite, reassure, ego boost, and anything else necessary for surviving and thriving. Everyone and everything depends on you feeling safe and secure together. If you have children, they will depend on the two of you to remain in love, be good caregivers to each other, and be good examples of how a love relationship works.

What they see and learn from you will determine how they go forward in life with their own relationships.

What's Your Shared Vision for Your Relationship?

Having a shared vision for your collaboration is an important first step in creating a secure-functioning relationship. One way to create a shared vision is to sit with your partner and talk through what each of you envisions in a happy marriage and long-term partnership. Each of you make a list of what the guiding principles of this relationship should be. Whatever you list, you must be willing to do for your partner. No double standards unless you agree to a double standard. For instance, you want your partner to always be chivalrous and open doors for you, and you have *agreed* on the fact that this effort is made by only one of you.

Here are some questions to get you started; provide specifics when possible:

- What's our highest priority? Relationship? Work? Independence?

- How do we handle distress with each other?

- How do we settle our differences?

- How do we make important decisions?

- How do we get each other to do things we may not want to do?

- How do we handle competing or intruding people, things, tasks? Think exes, parents, friends, work, hobbies, drugs or alcohol, and so forth.

- How do we manage shared labor such as housework, shopping, bills, kids, and so forth?

- How do we keep romantic love alive?

- How do we manage conflict?

- How do we repair, apologize, or make amends for hurting each other? How long should it take to fix injuries?

- How do we protect each other in private and in public?

SHARED PRINCIPLES OF GOVERNANCE EXAMPLES

- We put our relationship first.

- We have each other's back.

- We protect each other in public and in private.

- If one of us is in distress, we drop what we're doing and minister to that partner.

I can't stress enough the importance of forming shared principles of governance. Consider them your "ten commandments" and treat them as such. These principles must remain pithy (think "Thou shalt not kill"), fully understood, and accepted as representing a deep and abiding personal belief. If you don't or can't fulfill your side of these agreements under all circumstances, then the guiding principles don't truly exist. Take this very seriously and make certain your principles are in accord with each other.

SECURE OR INSECURE FUNCTIONING?

Consider a few examples of what secure functioning is *not*. Charlotte and Austin are planning to get married. Except for the time he proposed, Austin isn't in the habit of telling Charlotte he loves her. She thinks this is just a "guy thing," but although she loves him and enjoys their coupledom, she worries about whether he's as committed to their relationship as she is. In addition to feeling unsure of how he feels about her, Charlotte feels insecure about their future together.

When Josh comes home, he wants to share his day with Arya. When they married a year ago, they talked about sharing their lives in that way. But now he finds that Arya is always heading out the door for a run when he gets home. She says she needs that to unwind from her own day. Sometimes they share later, but often it doesn't happen. Josh feels unsupported, as if he's still going through life on his own.

One more. When Taylor and Jake were out with friends, she liked feeling his arm around her even while he was talking to his buddy. But then he teased her about having a second dessert and speculated that she wouldn't fit into her wedding gown. "Hey, that's not cool," she said. He assured her it was all in fun, but she was embarrassed. She felt hurt and insecure about whether she could count on Jake to protect her in public.

GETTING IT RIGHT FROM THE START

If you consider yourselves a survival unit, it will help you get things in perspective and also give you a sense of priority. As a survival unit, what's most important? Is your survival unit a luxury or necessity? Ensure continuous, mutual survival first. If either of you feels unsafe, insecure, or untrusting, thriving will take a back seat. This is especially true for the human primate. We *know* that when the human attachment system is insecure, personal and mutual development will stall, just as it does in infancy and childhood. You can't thrive—that is, grow, develop toward higher complexity as a creative, productive, and socially advanced human being—if your sense of safety and security in your primary attachment relationship is compromised.

The most important reason to marry is to become a thriving survival unit. Marriage for the sake of marriage is akin to planting a garden in quicksand. Other aspects such as passion, common interests, and the desire to have children become less important over time. Ultimately, if you want a relationship that stands the test of time, marry knowing your number one reason is to create a secure-functioning, thriving partnership.

2

HOW STRONG IS YOUR
COUPLE BUBBLE?

One indication of a secure-functioning relationship, and thus a prerequisite for a successful marriage, is the ability to create a couple bubble, through which the partners can face the world together. A couple bubble is a self-generating energy system that provides resources and protection to the couple. The term *couple bubble* was cocreated by Marion Solomon and me around 2008, which I describe in detail in *Wired for Love: How Understanding Your Partner's Brain and Attachment Style Can Help You Defuse Conflict and Build a Secure Relationship.*[1] Imagine a couple bubble as a terrarium with its own ecosystem that provides sustenance for its inhabitants, in which each partner is a steward of this ecosystem, a guardian of the atmosphere, water, air, and lushness of the growth that takes place.

The couple bubble is a place of rest, relaxation, and restoration; a place to be fully yourself. It's a place for vitality, encouragement, and full faith in your partner, as well as for understanding, compassion, and forgiveness. Sound too idealistic? Unattainable? I wouldn't be so cynical just yet. In a strong couple bubble partners take existential fears and concerns off the table and never threaten the existence of the relationship. Partners understand the mayhem that's unleashed under such conditions of doubt and worry. Tremendous internal resources are squandered by partners who play with this particular fire, resources that would be better put toward self-improvement, creativity, and productivity.

We know the human primate suffers greatly when insecurely attached to a "primary" caregiver. What's the point of maintaining such insecurity? One reason might be to use it as leverage to get our partner to submit in some manner. But that's a dangerous weapon to wield because it causes the earth to shake beneath each partner. Auditioning (for a permanent commitment) must end at some point. When we take our chances and leap into the unknown, resources are freed up for other important decisions and activities. Partners who have a couple bubble understand this and have taken ambivalence, doubt, and auditioning off the table. Next!

In your couple bubble, you accept each other as is and regard each other as the best thing since sliced turkey. Why? Because your self-esteem is in constant flux given the slings and arrows of every-day life. Imagine if in your family home, your parents looked at you with continuous disappointment, disregard, or disdain. How would your self-esteem be? Would you want to stay in this home? To do so would be self-harming. So why would you devalue the person you have chosen to be your most important person? Lift your partner up or they will underperform for you. Secure functioning means that you both have put all your money, all your bets, on the other.

Here's an important distinction that should be made before going further. In our couple bubble, Tracey and I take care in how we behave toward each other. Do we have critical thoughts about each other? You betcha. Do we sometimes wish the other would do something differently? Of course. Yet we both understand the difference between inside and outside our heads. If I were to confuse the internal flotsam and jetsam of my mind with my duty as Tracey's partner to consistently treat her with respect and high regard, we wouldn't be secure functioning. I would compromise our couple bubble each time I exposed Tracey to all my internal ups, downs, and sideways. There's a difference between letting Tracey in on how my mind works and making her responsible for every negative thought that crosses my mind.

I've seen this mistake all too often in my clinic. A partner continually confuses inside with outside and externalizes their internal critical self, or ambivalent self, or anxious self, or angry self, or devaluing self . . . so that their internal mayhem creates an enormous disturbance in the couple bubble. I consider this a massive sign of immaturity and a definite sign of a one-person psychological system. Remember, secure functioning is a two-person psychological system. When one person continually makes their partner a proxy for their internal conflicts they're not doing the couple bubble thing. A couple bubble is all about us, and we're both wardens of this ecosystem. If one of us pollutes the environment we both suffer.

So just how strong is your bubble? Explore the questions below.

DO YOU KNOW HOW TO COLLABORATE?

Doing things together, especially things you both enjoy, can strengthen your couple bubble. Tracey and I used to rock climb (indoors only) and found it to be a remarkable couple activity. I was interviewed by *Men's Health* magazine about the cooperative nature of rock climbing, a sport that encourages partners to collaborate and work together. A good rock climbing gym is often filled with couples, especially in the evening. No wonder. The music is blasting, and partners are entirely focused on each other as one climbs and the other body belays—ready to catch their falling partner from crashing onto the floor (or worse). This takes focus, concentration, and trust. In outdoor climbing, as in life, the risks are much higher and the conditions are variable. Partners must find intricate and attuned ways to communicate with each other. Their lives depend on this. They must also prepare for all foreseeable problems. If you can imagine what this takes—the collaboration, cooperation, communication—then you have a great metaphor for secure functioning within a strong couple bubble.

As you learned in chapter 1, partners are collaborative and cooperative in secure-functioning relationships. One of the ways I can tell if a couple is collaborative is by having them tell me a story, as if I'm a dinner guest. I ask them to talk about the vacation they recently took, how they met, and so on. I will often pick a subject around which they disagree and see how they perform this task—two people speaking with a single narrative voice. Noncollaborative partners will interrupt and correct each other, roll their eyes when the other speaks, interject something such as "Well, I have a different version," or offer some other verbal or nonverbal message that suggests they're not in accord. At some point I will say, "Oh boy. I'm beginning to feel uncomfortable. Please start over."

Sooner or later the couple will start looking at each other as they tell the story. That's what I'm looking for—eye contact. As they tell the story together they have to keep an eye on each other so that they get their story straight. The purpose of this exercise isn't to give phony eye-to-eye contact to impress the guest. Rather, it's to genuinely look to each other, listen to each other, as they tell their story in a unified manner. As a couple, we don't ordinarily get feedback about ourselves unless solicited. Even still, we may not actually get the full truth. Couples in my office will see themselves doing this on video. Video playback has a very intense effect on people's reality. It often feels like a slap in the face to watch and hear themselves interact unskillfully with their partner.

Another way I can tell that partners aren't collaborating is by how they talk in the therapy session. Do they focus on the relationship or do they focus solely on their individual needs? Partners who focus solely on their individual needs aren't collaborative. They're simply taking a stand for their own interests. I can't emphasize how important this last point is. Partners are either working together, first and foremost, on the relationship and then, secondarily, on all other matters, or they're not.

Here's an example of good cooperation and collaboration. Eda and Phillip began early to default to their respective skill sets, which turned out to be fairly complementary. Eda is very good at organizing and Phillip is good at bringing people together. Neither is particularly good at finances, so they outsource that skill to a money manager and accountant. They enjoy entertaining, traveling, music, and hiking. While Eda does most of the planning, she runs everything by Phillip, who either gives the go-ahead or suggests something else. If he should complain later, Eda simply brings up the fact that he signed on to the deal. Eda isn't the kind of person who stays in touch with people, so Phillip plans nights out or entertaining guests at home. And, like Eda, he runs the invitee list past Eda in order to get approval. Since they naturally move to their areas of expertise and comfort level, neither partner complains much.

Here's an example of bad cooperation and collaboration. Nicki and Eugene both have demanding careers. They've moved in together, and Nicki complains that Eugene just comes home and vegges out in front of the TV. "He thinks I should do all the cooking and cleaning. I have a job too," Nicki says. "If this is how it's going to be, I don't want it."

Eugene counters, "Okay, I understand that doesn't seem fair, but I'm bringing in most of the money here. I pay the majority of the bills. Nicki makes money, sure, but it's only enough to cover her basic expenses. Since I'm making most of the money, I think I should be spared most of the housework."

Though Eugene makes a good point about the ratio of income to expected household chores, it's never going to sound collaborative to anyone except, perhaps, a roommate. Nicki's not that. It also conveys a spirit of one-person-system thinking, as in, it's good to be king. Now, if Eugene and Nicki made an agreement that division of household chores would be based on income, that could work. I don't really believe it's a good idea, but secure functioning isn't what I think is fair and just, it's what *partners* consider fair and just.

The problem with Eugene and Nicki is their attitudes toward collaboration. If Eugene were to be fully cooperative, he'd simply get up out of his TV chair and help Nicki. If Nicki were to expect collaboration, she'd turn off the TV and tell him to help her. If he didn't, she'd have a sit-down with him about the continuance of the relationship based on his attitude of noncooperation.

Bean counting—tracking who did what and when—is another way couples show a lack of collaboration. Partners who have little or no faith in fairness will become miserly with tasks, chores, and money. Constant vigilance as to who is doing what, getting what, and losing what will strain any relationship, let alone a romantic alliance. If, indeed, there's a history of unfairness in the relationship, the attitude is more understandable. Still, the obsessive components of bean counting must stop if the relationship is to succeed. Secure functioning is supposed to free up resources, not tie them up. If you really don't trust the person you're with, why are you with them? If that person abused mutuality by months or years of inequity, fire them! Although, what were you doing all that time? Tolerating that behavior? Remember, in couples, where there's one, there's the other. No angels, no devils. Coconspirators, yes?

A Matter of Fairness

I've seen many a "gray divorce"* whereby wives leave their husbands for good and never take up another love relationship again. These women have had it. Done. The chronic inequity broke any desire for romantic relationships. Speaking of which, we should talk at least a little about the changing roles of male-female marriage. Role designations as they relate to divisions of responsibility do apply in gay and lesbian relationships, but the historic role assignments given to men and women over the millennia seem to remain a problem in modern marriages. This issue is strongly related to the matter of collaboration.

Too much unfairness, as experienced subjectively by either partner, eventually leads to increased threat with partners drifting away from the relationship. No good or bad deed goes unreturned. Accrue too much unfairness due to lack of cooperation and collaboration and get ready to pay the price.

Collaborative Narratives

Next time you go out to dinner with another couple, or when you find yourselves in public with friends or strangers, pay attention to how you tell a story together. Can you tell the story with a single narrative, telling it with give-and-take? Do you look to each other for cues and handoffs while you're telling the story?

Try telling a story together about something involving conflict between the two of you. Perhaps it's a story of your last vacation that went south. Can you tell the story in a way that doesn't embarrass either of you, make you sound like horrible people, or make your guests uncomfortable? Can you tell any of the stories without flat-out disagreeing with each other? This is a skill worth learning. Collaborative narratives force the two of you to work

---

*Gray divorce is a phenomenon of the baby boom generation whereby long-lasting relationships end in divorce when partners are in their mid- to late sixties and early seventies.

together while considering your friends and company. It also forces the two of you to modify history in a way that makes you both come out as champions.

DO YOU KNOW HOW TO ENGAGE IN COMMON ACTIVITIES?

When a couple approaches a common activity differently (in this case, attending a party), they will often take the option to distance themselves from each other and engage in separate activities because they can't master these situations together as a couple. Secure-functioning couples engage rather than avoid or distance themselves from each other.

Bob and Ted get into fights whenever they go to parties together. Actually, the fights occur *after* the party ends. Bob is shy, but Ted is outgoing. When they go to events, Ted typically abandons Bob and then complains that Bob doesn't interact with others in these situations. Bob will isolate at parties, and Ted believes this attracts attention, which embarrasses him. Bob is considering staying at home for future events. This is a mistake.

One of my colleagues, Allison Howe, came up with this mnemonic for dealing with situations that commonly cause problems: PaPeR (Predict, Plan, Repair). For Bob and Ted, the predicting and planning phases take place just before entering the party. Any earlier than that, they risk behaving reflexively and automatically, thereby getting into trouble. First, let's look at what not to do.

> **Bob** [after the party] Next time we go out, I want you to be more aware of me, to ask me how I'm doing and to make eye contact from time to time. We're a couple, remember?
>
> **Ted** Okay.

What's the problem with this strategy? Ted will never remember this. He will do what he does automatically just as Bob will do what he does automatically. This kind of preparation or planning is bound to get them both into trouble. So let's do it correctly, shall we?

[Parked in front of the house where the party is, Bob and Ted predict and plan.]

Bob   Before we go in, let's come up with a plan. I know you like to socialize and I'm okay with that. But I'd like you to stay with me for a while, hold my hand, and introduce me to people. Let's agree to check in with each other by just making eye contact. Okay?

Ted   Sure. I'm happy to do that.

Bob   Thank you. Also, let's agree on what time we'll leave. If I feel like staying after that, fine. But if I really need to go, I want you to respect that. I'll come up to you and whisper in your ear. Okay?

Ted   Okay. Let's say 10:00 p.m. I have to be up early anyway. How's that?

Bob   That's fine. Promise me, though, you won't give me a hard time if I want to leave at 10:00 p.m.

Ted   I won't. I promise. While we're at it, if you see me standing and talking with Jim, check in with me. He's really hard to get away from. You might come over and say something like, "Excuse me, I need to borrow Ted for moment."

Bob   Sure! I'd be happy to do that.

What happens after they apply PaPeR? Not only is the party experience successful for both of them but there's also no fight after the party or the next day. Nothing to look back on begrudgingly because they took care of business in the moment. So what about the repair part, the last step in the process? Ted didn't visually check in with Bob as much as Bob had expected. Knowing this, Ted apologizes to him on the way home.

Ted   I'm aware that I didn't make enough eye contact with you during the party. I'm really sorry. This is all new for me.

Bob   Thank you for that. I really appreciate it.

By repairing quickly with Bob, Ted saved himself a lot of problems. If Bob was upset about the lack of visual contact, Ted beat him to the punch by making a repair. If Bob wasn't upset, Ted earned himself a bunch of points by demonstrating his awareness.

Like Bob and Ted, we all have obligations and parties to attend. Go beyond obligations and find endeavors that you both enjoy and spend time doing them together. It doesn't have to be something death-defying or expensive to strengthen your bond. You can take a class together, work in the garden, or collaborate on a project. Over time you will create lots of positive long-term memories that will shore up your couple bubble.

DO YOU TAKE RESPONSIBILITY FOR HOW YOU'RE DIFFICULT?

Yes, all people are annoying and difficult, and yes, people's difficult sides are most likely to be on display within a love relationship. Yet as a secure-functioning couple trying to create a healthy couple bubble, it's important to be as easy to get along with as possible. Since you're a two-person psychological system, being unnecessarily difficult will only blow back on you. Here's an example.

James becomes sullen at times and has difficulty getting out of his funk. Marla understands that James is simply doing what he sometimes does automatically. She cues him by saying, "Okay, enough with the moodiness. We're going out in a few minutes. Attitude change, my sweets."

James, knowing that he tends to brood, responds to Marla's cue. Perhaps he talks about why he's feeling down, but he doesn't act it out, especially after Marla's cue. Similarly, Marla can talk sometimes with an overbearing vocal tone. She's unaware of this, as it's an automatic behavior, and she tends to do this when discussing business or political matters. Since Marla has agreed her tone can become a problem for others, he gently cues her with a calming hand movement on her thigh, especially when they're in public. She gets it and she doesn't resist, defend, or become difficult for James.

How are you difficult? Are there things you do that tick off others, times when you demand your way, areas in which you refuse to compromise? Do you fight fair? Withdraw when your partner needs to talk? Or talk so much that you keep your partner from participating? Do you use tears, threats, or temper tantrums to get your way? Do you overintellectualize? Use humor inappropriately? Hold grudges? Give up too easily?

You can keep your couple bubble intact by being honest about the ways in which your difficult behavior can affect your relationship and by learning to put the brakes on before the tension escalates.

EXERCISE
How Are You Difficult?

Think about how you can be difficult. Write it down. Ask your partner to do the same. When finished, get together, share what you wrote, and talk about it. Again, be honest. Don't confuse giving yourself a compliment with providing you and your partner with truth about yourself. Here are some examples of fake self-critique:

- "I care too much about people."

- "I give too much."

- "I think of others too much and not myself."

- "I don't let people do things for me."

- "I'm too sentimental."

There's nothing more annoying than to hear someone critique themselves with compliments. It makes them sound self-aggrandizing. Even worse, they come off as unaware of themselves and difficult. Everyone is difficult! Even easygoing people are often conflict avoidant or passive-aggressive. So come on! Get yourself in the mud and have some fun with this.

Things to consider:

- Do you brood?

- Do you throw tantrums?

- Do you refuse to take no for an answer?

- Do you have a hard time letting things go?

- Are you stubborn?

- Are you prideful to a fault?

- Do you have to be right?

- Do you have to get your way?

- Do you hold on to grudges?

- Do you have a hard time shifting from one emotional state to another?

- Do you avoid conflict?

- Do you seek conflict?

- Do you blame others for things you do?

- Do you tend to be negativistic? A complainer?

These are just some ideas to get you started. Once you've made these lists and shared them with each other, discuss proactive ways you can adjust any behavior that endangers your couple bubble. As you get better at secure functioning, you can agree to give and receive cues from each other for certain situations to avoid or de-escalate distress.

ARE YOU COMMITTED TO REMAINING GIRLFRIEND AND BOYFRIEND?

Your committed relationship may be with a person of the opposite sex or the same sex. I'll use an example of girlfriend and boyfriend. If you plan to become husband and wife, keep in mind that you must continue to be girlfriend and boyfriend. If you go on to be mother and father, you most definitely need to stay girlfriend and boyfriend. Why? "Husband and wife" has a certain meaning to it, as does "mother and father." The roles not only come with a full set of matching baggage but these titles also don't signify the juice that brought you together in the first place. So take a cue from the most successful couples. Even those in their seventies and eighties act as girlfriend and boyfriend forever. They get it! There's something so special about the beginning of a relationship and keeping that alive. Be romantic, gaze lovingly into each other's eyes, and plan date nights, adventures, and any other experiences that will keep those feelings of new love alive and strong.

ARE YOU CONFIDENT WITH EACH OTHER OR WALKING ON EGGSHELLS?

A secure-functioning couple is made up of partners who are unafraid of each other; they don't feel fear, apprehension, or intimidation around each other, and they don't walk on eggshells. If your partner seems to be cautious around you, it may signal that they don't feel comfortable being their true self and sharing the good, bad, and ugly. Often this is a sign that your partner feels threatened on some level, and you should at least be alerted to potential danger. Remember, the relationship is what you both say it is. If either of you believe the relationship can't withstand who you both really are, then, by your own admission, it's true. The relationship will be fear- and shame-based and there will be secrets. This avoidance also indicates that you haven't fully accepted each other, which, again, is central in a secure-functioning relationship. In general, if the relationship is so fragile that it can't tolerate the messiness of each partner, including missteps and stupid mistakes, the relationship will crumble.

IMPORTANT REMINDER

As I mentioned in chapter 1, it's important to differentiate between big T and small t threat. If your partner is
violent or abusive, that's the big T kind of threat. GET OUT
NOW! Seek help immediately and forget about this book
until you're safe.

But here's another reason not to walk on eggshells. When you hesitate
to share what's on your mind, as if you're afraid of what's going to
come out, you increase the chances that your partner will misunderstand your meaning. As you stumble to speak, your partner is filling
in the gaps. Do you really want your partner to make things up in
their head? As you will learn in the next chapter, our brains tend to
go negative. So be direct and keep it short. Say what you want to say
without padding the truth or beating around the bush. Not getting to
the point right away will get you into a fight, especially when the two
of you are in distress.

DO YOU HAVE A SHARED
SENSE OF HUMOR?

Humor is the great leveler and the great regulator. Without a sense
of humor the couple system can become rigid, overly serious, and
brittle. On the other hand, if either of you can't stand the other's
sense of humor, reconsider marriage. That's not going to play well
in the long run. As you might imagine, partners who share a sense
of humor and can laugh together are going to ride the waves of life
better than others. But it's not just having a sense of humor that's
important. The key is, does your partner find you funny? If they
don't, you might as well not have a sense of humor at all.

There have been many studies on partners who share a sense of
humor and those who don't. In one study, the relationships where men
found their female partners funny were more stable than the reverse.[2]
That doesn't mean that it's not important for him to also have a good

sense of humor. It may be that men are better with female partners who make them laugh because men tend to be a little bit more uptight.[*]

Some individuals make people laugh (producers) while others enjoy laughing (appreciators), and some are both producers and appreciators. Which are you? What about your partner? Of course, if you're a producer and your partner doesn't appreciate your humor, that can be quite deflating. This lack of appreciation can become a deal breaker for some folks.

Another problem is sensitivity to certain types of humor. Some people are attracted to dark humor, gallows humor, silly humor, or sick humor. It's problematic when your partner finds your humor offensive, insulting, or disgusting. Never make your partner the butt of your jokes. This will elicit an emotional response, which many partners will perceive as a threat. Even if your partner takes it in stride, that kind of humor isn't only denigrating but it will also undermine your couple bubble over time. If your partner's humor is offensive or hurtful, it's time to have a sit-down and talk about this issue. Alan and his fiancée, Elizabeth, had this exchange:

> **Alan** Everyone in my family jokes like this. Don't be so sensitive.
>
> **Elizabeth** [with stern resoluteness] I find that kind of humor offensive. I can't be party to that kind of insensitivity. It's abhorrent and racist and misogynistic.
>
> **Alan** Well that's who I am. I'm not going to suddenly change my sense of humor to suit your tastes. Besides, I'm not making fun of you. Lighten up, why don't you?

---

[*] Men have nervous systems that climb higher and faster and stay pitched longer than women. There seems to be an evolutionary purpose behind this. Men, in protecting the clan from predators, need to be aroused quickly by sounds, movement, or aggressive behavior so they can fight off intruders or attackers. And they must stay ready if the predator should return. While we're on the subject, this may also be why men tend to have a lower, booming voice. That loud booming voice tends to stop approaching movement and also is intended to scare off attackers. Women's voices tend to be higher pitched, like a siren, to pull family members together in a huddle for safety.

If this sounds at all familiar to you, there may be trouble ahead. Can we change Alan? I don't think it's likely. Can we change Elizabeth? I don't think that's likely either. Many times in my clinic I've seen partners with wildly different takes on what is and isn't funny. And I've never experienced either person shift their position.

EXERCISE
Can You Make Each Other Laugh?

Try your hand at making your partner laugh. Make a funny face or offer a funny joke or quip about something you share. Some couples are good at rough-and-tumble humor. They poke and prod each other, sometimes using sarcasm, other times sparring because they find it fun. Secure-functioning partners who do rough-and-tumble know how to keep it from going too far. Tracey and I sometimes give each other the finger. We're both fine with this and it makes us both laugh. It's a way to express our displeasure without being serious about it. We know what we can and can't do without crossing a line, which is important for you too.

Dos and Don'ts Regarding Humor

- DO try lots of different ways to make your partner laugh.

- DO explore your partner's sense of humor. What do they find funny?

- DO find out what definitely isn't funny to your partner.

- DO find out what's offensive to your partner.

- DO find out if your partner is a *producer* of humor, an *appreciator* of humor, or both.

- DON'T continue to joke about things that aren't funny to your partner.

- DON'T make jokes at your partner's expense.

- DON'T tickle your partner.

LEARN HOW TO BROKER WIN-WIN OUTCOMES

Part of operating as a two-person system is understanding that you're with someone who has a different point of view than yours. You also understand that in order for the two of you to move together, it can't be at one person's cost. This is one of the frustrations of working on any team. One has to remember that your interests aren't always in accord with the others, and therefore adjustments must be made. Thankfully, collaborative partners will create outcomes that are good for both of them, not just for one. So how is this done?

One-Person Orientation Versus Two-Person Orientation

This is a good time to introduce the concepts of one-person and two-person orientations. In a one-person model, a partner will put their individual needs before the relationship's needs (and before their partner's needs). Although some see this as a sign of independence—I can do my thing and you can do yours—it's really a sign of pseudoautonomy. The paradigm: As long as I get my needs met, I will work toward getting your needs met. And if mine aren't met, you're out of luck. If you still question whether a one-person model is fair, remember that when *your* needs aren't being met, your partner won't see that as a concern.

In a two-person model, the needs of the relationship come first, where neither partner will agree on a solution that will come at the expense of the other. Secure-functioning relationships are two-person psychological systems where both parties feel respected, heard, and safe. The partners' wagons are hitched together. As a survival-based partnership, it's a matter of mutually assured survival and thriving as well as mutually assured destruction. Finding solutions that are mutually agreeable protects and strengthens the couple bubble. Many people hear this concept of mutuality and think they have to give up what they want or "compromise," which has a negative connotation in many vernaculars. I prefer the word *bargaining* instead of *compromising*. In a bargain, both may need to give something to get something. In the end, both enjoy a better outcome.

Here's an example from a page in Lila and Marty's history book, where neither win and neither is concerned with the other's needs:

> **Lila** We disagree about where to go for vacation. I want to go to Hawaii but you're tired of Hawaii and want to go to Italy instead.
>
> **Marty** [angrily] I get to do what I want to do every now and then, don't I? I'm the wage earner. If I want to go to Italy and have us meet my distant relatives, we'll go to Italy!
>
> **Lila** What do you think I do all day, Mr. Wage Earner? Sit around and eat ice cream while you do the heavy lifting? Think about all *I* do for this family. We can go to Italy anytime, but I want to relax in Hawaii.

Let's look at how the same scene would play out in a secure-functioning partnership:

> **Lila** I know you're tired of going to Hawaii and you've wanted me to see Italy and meet your relatives. But I don't want to go to Italy during the summer because it's sweltering hot.
>
> **Marty** It's hot in Hawaii during the summer too, so what's the difference?
>
> **Lila** I agree with you [laughing at his logic]. Look, I understand how much you've wanted to go to Italy and that I haven't been flexible. I also understand that you're tired of Hawaii and want to go someplace new with me and the children. Is it possible for us to go to Italy at a time when

it's not so hot and to make parts of the trip as
relaxing as it is in Hawaii?

Marty [thinking for a moment] Hmm. That would be fine
except that the children are only out of school in
the summer.

Lila That's a good point, and I can't think of a solution."
[Lila's feeling a bit stuck.]

Marty How about this? This trip, we could go to northern
Italy near the Alps where it's cooler and take a
day trip to Naples to see my family. That way, we
would spend only one or two days in the heat.

TIP

It's important to offer something up when turning something down. Secure functioning involves bargaining and a
back-and-forth. It's unhelpful and noncollaborative to say
no to something without offering anything else in its stead.

Lila [thinking] That's a great idea except for the part
that we'll be moving around a lot and that
doesn't sound very relaxing.

Marty I would like it if you went with me and the kids
to Naples. I'm offering you more than a week to
relax up north. What if you stay up there while I
take the kids south for a few days?
[A moment of silence ensues.]

Marty I can tell you don't like these ideas.

Lila I'm sorry. I know you're trying to make it work for
me. Can we drop this for a bit, so I can think
about it a while?

Marty [enthusiastically] Sure. Let's go get the kids from
soccer practice.

They agree to table the discussion and move on to something less stressful. They haven't come up yet with a win-win solution but, because they have a track record of creating win-wins, neither is unhappy.

Later that day Lila offers another solution.

> **Lila** How about we all go to Naples and Rome and Sorento, which are by the water, and take at least two days to just relax, maybe go sightseeing in the evening when it's cooler?"
>
> **Marty** [with a bright smile] You got it! And we can go to Hawaii in the fall, just the two of us, when the kids are back in school. How's that?
> [Lila hugs and kisses Marty.]
>
> **Lila** [looking into Marty's eyes] I love you. I love how we always work these things out.

All couples face similar situations, and many find it difficult to broker win-win outcomes. It's all too easy to become stubborn and self-centered, to dig in our heels or grow frustrated. Some partners might say that the back-and-forth isn't worth it, and they avoid it by considering separate trips. But that's a lazy solution that leads to distancing and drift. Rather than expect you will either want the same thing or someone has to capitulate, consider a third option: bargain! Make it good for both of you: "How about we do this?" or "What about if I do this for you?"

If you say no to an offer, you had better come up with a counteroffer, otherwise you will (and should) be considered uncooperative and noncollaborative. You're part of a team. Just turning something down without offering an alternative is flat-out unhelpful and annoying. Lila decided to take some time to formulate a bargain instead of just refusing. If both of you see this as a two-person problem-solving task, you will get through it successfully. If one or both of you see problem solving as the other person's undertaking, that's not secure functioning.

Come to a Win-Win Decision

I want the two of you to make a decision around something you disagree on. Maybe it's about a vacation. Perhaps it's about where you want to live or where to go for dinner. Now get something with a timer you can set.

Here are the rules: You only have fifteen minutes and you have to come to a win-win solution, even if it's just for the time being. You can always come back to the table on any agreement you make. This means you will have to avoid distractions, branching off into irrelevant subtopics, and shrugging your shoulders.

DO YOU USE ATTRACTION INSTEAD OF FEAR, THREAT, GUILT, OR SHAME?

Secure-functioning partners favor using attraction to get what they want. By attraction, I don't mean physical attractiveness. Rather, I mean playfulness, seduction, persuasion, bargaining, cajolery, and enticement. The use of fear, threat, guilt, or shame will only breed acrimony between you. The skillful use of attraction requires creativity, cleverness, cunning, and finesse. It's also a necessary skill set for brokering win-win results between partners.

A big part of coupledom involves doing things together because you *want to*, not because you *have to*. How good are you at getting your partner to *want* to do something? How clever can you be? Are you a [your partner's name] whisperer? If you've ever watched a horse, dog, or cat "whisperer," you know they never beat the animal into submission, nor do they use fear, threat, or any other coercive tactic to change behavior. I'm sure you've seen people lash out when they feel helpless, powerless, and ineffectual. They turn to aggression, avoidance, or indifference. You and your partner are in each other's care, you're each other's master. What kind of master will you be?

There's a scene from the 2002 hit comedy *My Big Fat Greek Wedding* in which Maria (played by Lainie Kazan) must get her husband, Kosta (played by Michael Constantine), to do something he wouldn't otherwise suggest by tricking him into thinking it's his own idea. She jokes to her daughter that while Kosta is the head of the family, she's the neck and can get Kosta to see things her way by turning him ever so slightly. I know some may call this trickery or underhanded behavior, but it's their way of creating balance in their relationship, where both parties win.

Is it fair to be strategic with your partner? It's not only fair but also highly skillful. Some might say it's manipulative. But consider this: everyone manipulates. Manipulation is looked down upon when it's at another person's cost, and I would never suggest that. I hope you can see that *how* you get your partner to do something you want makes all the difference when it comes to secure functioning.

EXERCISE
Beckoning

You and your partner should stand several feet away from each other, perhaps even across the room. One of you is the beckoner and the other is being beckoned. Face each other and don't talk. Here are the rules:

- The beckoner must get the other partner to come to them.

- Neither partner can talk.

- The beckoner can do anything except go get the partner. Remember, the partner must be beckoned.

- The beckoned partner moves only if really persuaded, not because they feel sorry for the beckoning partner. No pity walking.

Notice how long it takes for your partner to come to you. What made the beckoned partner move? What didn't work? Did the beckoner become frustrated? Did the beckoner appear attractive to the other partner? Did the beckoner use anything that could be interpreted as fear, threat, guilt, or shame? Did the beckoner feel comfortable beckoning? Did they look comfortable?

Now do the exercise again with partners playing the same roles, only this time the beckoner must use a different tactic. Let's see how many tricks are in that bag. Again, what worked, what didn't, and why? Switch positions and do this again.

Getting Your Partner to Come Home

Here's a fun exercise to see if you're good at getting your partner to come home if and when you want them to. There's a catch, though. You can't use yourself in any way in the "I" sense, such as "I want you," "I want you to come home," or "I need you to be here." And you can't use fear, threat, or guilt, such as "Something's wrong with the kids so come home right now"; "I'm not feeling well, I need you"; "The house is on fire"; "If you don't come home I'll know you don't love me"; or "Come home now or you'll regret it." Instead, you must use an enticement, bait, or something that will be so tempting that your partner will drop everything and come home.

Sit across from each other and maintain eye contact. Take turns floating an attraction, one at a time, so you can see it register on your partner's face and in their eyes. Did their face and eyes light up? Did their pupils dilate? Did you get an affirmative response?

Remember, you can't offer something you can't deliver upon. You will never be trusted again if you do. Your partner's response *must* be unequivocally charged with excitement. Don't make the offer long or confusing because you will get a false positive or negative. Don't add more than one enticement or the same problem will occur. Do this seriously. If you succeed, try another and then another. If you fail, don't give up . . . ever. There's *always* something that works. Knowing how to entice, seduce, excite, and lure your partner is an important skill to possess. Just giving up and letting your partner do what they want, when they want, isn't secure functioning.

Switch roles and let the other partner give it a try. Have fun with this.

DO YOU KNOW WHEN YOU CAN'T SAY NO?

A few things are absolute musts in the secure-functioning world. Missing a birthday and forgetting an anniversary come at heavy costs. You can make up for those, and hopefully you will. But there are certain things for which you can't make up no matter how hard you try. Once it's done, it's done; and it's remembered. Let's go through the list.

Being Unavailable When Your Partner Is Sick

When you're sick and your partner isn't attentive, you tend to remember. When we're sick, we're vulnerable, and we all get better and heal faster when we're comforted and cared for. Many people don't care whether they're attended to; some even resent the idea, preferring to retreat to bed until they feel better. Nonetheless, it doesn't change the fact that isolation when sick doesn't hasten wellness. There are many ways we can show up for our partner when they're ill; for example, checking in to ask what feels best—whether that be cooking for them, reading to them, getting them healing aids, or simply providing love and company.

Being Unavailable When Your Partner Is in the Hospital or Facing Bad News from a Doctor

Being in the hospital is also a vulnerable time—even more so, because we're without the comforts of home. If you're too busy to be there with your partner, or you're nonchalant about your partner's distress, it will leave an indelible impression. It's also likely to start a firestorm of complaints about neglect. In the attachment world, not showing up for your partner at the hospital, being inattentive, or acting resentful is a big fat no-no because it goes right to the heart of safety and security. If you can't show up for your partner who is in the hospital, getting bad news from a doctor, or going through a tough procedure or surgery, then what good are you? And what's the point of the relationship? A Saint Bernard would surely be more useful.

Being Unavailable When There's a Family Funeral to Attend

Not good if you don't accompany your partner to a close friend's or family member's funeral. Your partner may say that it's not a big deal or that your work is important or whatever. But don't you dare listen. Go to that funeral come hell or high water. If you don't, it's likely to cause a rift between you and your partner because you weren't there at a key life passage in your partner's life. In the attachment world, this is something you make time for.

Being Unavailable for Your Partner's Celebration or Event

In the attachment world, sharing a partner's celebration of a milestone or other achievement is up there with being available for soothing and comforting. If you're not there to witness and participate in your partner's successes and celebrations, the reason had better be that you're either trapped under heavy furniture or just simply dead.

DO YOU KNOW YOUR COMMON PURPOSE?

As I discussed in chapter 1, secure functioning means that your relationship exhibits interdependence, not dependence or codependence. Partners are at the top of the food chain but they're not all things to each other. Interdependence means that each partner has a stake in a common "something," such as to have enough money to live comfortably, to vanquish loneliness, to serve God, to have a family, or to make each other's lives better. Child-rearing is an obvious reason for interdependency, but it's often not used in that way. If both partners aren't fully in each other's care, they will see child-rearing as a separate one-person enterprise, not as a collaboration. There must be a sustaining reason for partners to exist over the long term interdependently, surviving and thriving together.

Your Couple Mission Statement

In Stephen Covey's marvelous audiobook *How to Develop Your Family Mission Statement*, he describes the importance of a family mission statement as vital to developing a shared notion of what the family should be.[3] I apply the same idea here to your couple mission statement. Don't rush this! Make the conversations a special time when you're both relaxed. Be completely open and honest with each other. Here are some questions you should ask each other:

- What defines you as a couple?

- What's your purpose as a couple? What or whom do you serve? What's the point of you two coming and staying together?

- What do you do for each other you couldn't pay someone to do? (Don't use "love" because you can actually pay someone for that.)

- What are you both most afraid of as a couple? Use that to come up with a positive principle in your mission statement.

- Where are you headed as a couple?

- What are you becoming as a couple?

- What are your core values?

- Should you be admired as a couple? If so, why? Are you the real deal or a performing couple?

To clarify further, a mission statement shapes our today. A vision statement prepares us for tomorrow. We can prepare for tomorrow if we believe in our values. See if you can come up with a succinct mission statement that even a child could understand. This could even be part of your commitment ceremony.

Mission Statements

GOOD STATEMENTS	BAD STATEMENTS
Are emotionally impactful	Are dry or hard to connect with
Are pithy and concise	Are rambling and too wordy
Are easy to understand	Are too complicated
Have broad implications	Are too narrow in scope
Are memorable	Are forgettable

Here's an example of a fine couple mission statement. I've altered it from its original, which was a family mission statement:

> To be partners who love and care for each other so that we can have a positive impact on our world. We commit to be there for each other and work together as a team. We resolve to be caring, helpful, encouraging, loving, loyal, to have a servant's heart, to enjoy each other, and to never give up.

There are other topics such as thirds, fighting well, and sex that can threaten your couple bubble. I've devoted a chapter to each to give you deeper insights. But first we will discuss your negative brain, which often causes unnecessary struggles and strife.

3

MANAGING YOUR
NEGATIVE BRAIN

In previous books I've said that our brains are more inclined for war than love, and part of what makes relationships so difficult is the "negative bias" of the brain. Because there's a lack of early education on how to manage our own brain, I'm teaching it here so you can take a load off yourself and your partner for mistakes the two of you *will* make because you're human and not because you're horrible people. After many years of counseling couples, I can say with all sincerity that most people are doing the best they can, with no intention to harm, even though it may often seem the opposite. We're memory-driven, automatic, and reflexive creatures who act and react at whirlwind speeds and therefore without thought. It's important to know and understand how the brain operates, how we store memories, and how our actions can frequently hurt others. Much of the time we take personally the actions and inactions of our partner when it's not at all personal or intended to create strife. Let's explore how the brain works, and how it plays into the distress all couples experience.

PRIMITIVES AND AMBASSADORS

For the sake of simplicity, imagine the brain is divided into two sections: primitives and ambassadors. As human beings, we need both our primitives and ambassadors to function properly to help us determine what's true and false. One without the other will mislead us.

The primitives are structures in the brain that are phylogenetically (and ontologically) older than the ambassadors. Our primitives develop earlier—prior to and during infancy—and require less oxygen and glucose (they're cheaper to run) to perform tasks due to fewer neurons in the primitive areas than the ambassador regions. Primitives are lightning fast and memory based, which allows for most functions to be performed automatically with the least amount of energy expenditure. The primitives, sometimes referred to as our automatic brain, are extremely vital to everyday function. They recognize danger, threat, attraction, familiarity, and so on, through the face, eyes, voice, gestures, movements, and even posture. The primitives, which we rely on for about 80 to 90 percent of what we do, are deeply hooked into sensorimotor operations. What we smell, taste, touch, see, hear, and feel are connected to this recognition.

Some ambassadors operate via thought, cognition, and reason but are also influenced by perceptions and emotions. Some ambassadors allow you to predict, plan, and solve problems. Other ambassadors perform error-correction functions to guard against mistakes of perception and calculation. Finally, most ambassadors function as regulators of emotions and impulses. Sounds terrific, right? One thing, though: ambassadors are much more "expensive" to run—they need more oxygen and glucose than primitives because they perform lots of fancy operations—and they're slower. As such, ambassadors require more time and energy to perform their tasks. With the experience of distress or threat, ambassador areas become underresourced, and processing time is reduced. Error-correction functions are compromised as your brain and body must act and react quickly, more automatically. Imagine standing on railroad tracks with a train speeding toward you. Do you really have time to calculate the train's speed and distance before it strikes you? Of course not. It's coming at you, fast, and you jump out of the way.

PRIMITIVES	AMBASSADORS
This region is cheap to run, quick, memory based, energy conserving, and automatic.	This region is expensive to run, slow, thought based, energy expending, inhibiting, restricting, error correcting, and regulating.
The primitives operate on recognition. Most of your day is run by your primitives, and most of what they do is without your knowledge or permission.	The ambassadors allow you to interpret. They perform functions, such as error-correct; regulate primitives; and predict, plan, and solve problems.

Sensory perceptions enter primitive areas first and are then processed by other structures that provide detail, dimension, meaning, and integration with other sense perceptions. Your emotional state is driven primarily by the primitives.

You might think of the rather imprecise location of ambassadors and primitives in terms of top to bottom and front to back, respectively. Please do understand that the use of these terms grossly simplifies an exquisitely complex system. Having now said that, allow me to include the left and right hemispheres of the brain.

Communication—with our bodies, faces, voices, and so on—involves both the ambassadors and primitives. However, the left and right hemispheres communicate differently, with the left side dominant for speech and language comprehension (explicit) and the right dominant for nonverbal (implicit) communication with others. Often these two forms of expression are at odds and can often show up as mismatched: "You said you're not angry, but you look angry."

The brain's left hemisphere is a "detailer" and sequencer. It fills in all the blanks from the right hemisphere, which makes it very good for confabulation (otherwise known as making shit up). It's a serial processor that takes and uses data bit by bit, which is why it's also good at logistics and deductive thinking. A left-leaning romantic partner is going to see the world through a lens of logic, precision, deduction, rationality, and reasoning.

The right hemisphere functions somewhat differently. For one thing, it develops before the left. For another, the right hemisphere is a mighty processor that takes in multiple streams of information, such as sensations and perceptions, quasi-simultaneously, like a parallel processor. It's very good at handling many things at once, including regulation systems of the brain and body, stress management, implicit memories, feelings and emotions, and facial recognition. Unlike the left hemisphere, the right takes in the gestalt but not the detail. Imagine Pablo Picasso's famous deconstruction of a bull in his lithograph series *Bull*. The bull, at its most basic and undefined, is what the right hemisphere "sees." The left sees a fully detailed, fleshed-out bull. Partners who are right-leaning tend to see the world through a lens of emotion and meaning and not with the same calculated precision of those who are left-leaning. The thing is, neither is more "right" than the other. Just different.

OUR NEGATIVE BRAIN

Our brain has a negativity bias so that, in the absence of positive interaction with others, it will always go negative: bad thoughts, fearful thoughts, aggressive thoughts, weird fantasies, hauntings, obsessions, and even madness. This is why solitary confinement is considered cruel and unusual punishment. The untrained mind alone isn't exactly Disneyland. In 1914, famed psychoanalyst Carl Jung experimented in exploring his unconscious. He went through a psychotic episode and later recommended that others should proceed with caution.[1] Without positive interactions with others, our brain tends to go negative. Without interaction, we're left alone with our mind, and that can lead us to unbridled fears, obsessions, anxieties, and aggression.

TIP

Mindfulness practices, particularly insight meditation, can be practiced to harness and understand the mind, and to become less prone to allowing one's own mind to be subjected to the hijinks perpetrated by the average brain.[2]

Want to see this negativity bias in action? Have your friend or lover look at you blankly while you talk or express your feelings. Their "neutral" face will appear negative to you in short order. Because your friend isn't sending signals or responding to your signals, your brain fills in the blanks from a low signaling, low expressive face and does it with flair. Ever notice that a shy person initially comes off as indifferent, arrogant, or judgmental? And when you get to know that person, they're none of those things? That's your brain making up stuff.

Another reason our brains are more warlike has to do with the number of structures devoted to keeping us alive and out of danger. So why should we care about this? Think about how easy it will be for you and your partner to become distressed over a misunderstanding.

NERVOUS SYSTEM REGULATION

What's key in secure-functioning relationships is arousal regulation. Here, *arousal* pertains only to our nervous system, which is actually several things. First, there's the central nervous system: our brain, brainstem, and spinal cord. Then there's the autonomic nervous system, a division of the peripheral nervous system that influences involuntary internal organ function, such as breathing, heart rate, all appetites, sexual function, pupil dilation, urination, digestion, and the fight-or-flight response.

The Four Regulation (Self-Care) Strategies

AUTOREGULATION	From birth	Self-stimulation and self-soothing without the need of another person
		No interpersonal stress experienced
		Can be dissociative or similar to overfocusing on a task
		EXAMPLES: Gaze averting, reading, painting, watching TV, masturbating, using street drugs and alcohol

EXTERNAL REGULATION	*From birth*	Interactive but in one direction at a time
		Lacks simultaneity (simultaneous interaction in both directions)
		Similar to codependent overfocusing on self or other
		EXAMPLES: Infant being cradled and soothed by caregiver, listening to an educational lecture, talking to a friend about your troubles or vice versa
INTERACTIVE REGULATION (a.k.a. coregulation, mutual regulation)	*From birth*	Both individuals regulating each other in real time
		Usually face to face and eye to eye (skin to skin, especially during childhood)
		Partners are in attunement
		Infants lead, caregivers follow, then the two both lead and follow
		EXAMPLES: Partners dancing together, lovemaking, partners engrossed in rewarding conversation, musicians playing together
SELF-REGULATION	*From ten to twelve months*	The only strategy that's inhibitory and restricting: frustration tolerance, impulse control, remaining socially engaged
		Executive function
		EXAMPLES: Managing one's own arousal through breath control, muscle relaxation, vocal control, maintaining friendly eye contact; desire and ability to communicate when under stress

The autonomic nervous system is split between two tracks. One, the sympathetic system, is excitatory; it's a quick-responding, mobilizing, energy-expending system. The other, the parasympathetic system, is inhibitory—slow and dampening. The sympathetic system is the accelerator; the parasympathetic is the brake. When I use the term *arousal* I'm referring to the extent to which these two branches are active. High arousal, or hyperarousal, refers to high sympathetic activation of the autonomic nervous system. Sympathetic emotions are joy, ecstasy, orgasm, lust, and bliss, as well as dissociative rage, terror, and mania. Low arousal, or hypoarousal, refers to parasympathetic activation, which includes relaxation, contemplation, repose, sadness, depression, shame, and dissociation.

When my arousal goes up, my breathing, heart rate, and blood pressure increase; my skin may flush, my muscles may tighten, my spine and neck may straighten, my fingers and toes may curl, my vocal pitch may be a bit higher, and everything about me is faster. When my arousal goes down, my skin may blanch, my muscles may loosen, and my shoulders may roll forward until I slump—everything about me is slower. My breathing, heart rate, and blood pressure decrease, and my vocal pitch may sound lower. If I drop too far, I can become nauseous and dizzy, with my ears ringing, until I faint. When arousal is at an optimal level, I'm relaxed *and* alert, neither in fight or flight (hyperaroused) nor collapsed (hypoaroused).

AROUSAL REGULATION AND COREGULATION OF EMOTIONAL STATES

Arousal regulation is a term that refers not to sexual arousal but to energetic, often emotional states ranging from mania to unconsciousness. It's the key to both pleasurable experiences—exciting love, quiet love, ecstasy, joy, and bliss—and threatening ones—hate, rage, terror, shame, depression, and life threat. Arousal regulation involves aspects of the autonomic and central nervous systems' reactions to internal and external stimuli that govern approach and withdrawal behaviors as well as fighting, fleeing, freezing, and fainting. So why is this important to coupling? Once partners begin to perceive the relationship as long term, they depend (nonconsciously) on each other for nervous system regulation, which means balancing each other's energy and emotion. Each couple is completely unique, a system unto its own and a mixture that can't be duplicated. These two nervous systems (a collection of memory, autonomic nervous system reactivity, social-emotional acuity, and brain function) either get along well or they don't.

Exciting Love

Understanding arousal allows you to feed your relationship. The sympathetic nervous system gives you your vitality, interest, and curiosity, and is important for experiencing *exciting love*, which is the addictive love experience. It's marked by high levels of dopamine, noradrenaline, and other fine hormones and neurotransmitters. It's generally achieved through direct eye-to-eye and skin-to-skin contact, but also when sharing novel experiences that stimulate excitement, such as traveling to new places. Lots of couples have difficulty cocreating exciting love, yet it's an essential mutual state that you and your partner can recreate, no matter how long you've been together.

EXERCISE
Making Eye Contact

One of the best ways to engender exciting love is to (1) make direct eye contact in close proximity (eye gazing), (2) mutually focus on an exciting third object, such as a novel location with beautiful scenery, to amplify the positive in each other, and (3) convert your own excitement so it can be shared by your mate, such as when you receive good news.

Sit across from each other and gaze into each other's eyes. Notice that as soon as you do, you get excited (either positively or negatively). That's your arousal going up. Unless eye contact is threatening to you or your partner, your arousal should settle down in a few minutes. Don't stare, but rather really look. Paint your partner's eyes with yours. You're now peering into each other's nervous systems!

- As you gaze into each other's eyes, take turns saying something loving and personal, including your partner's first name. For example: "Nancy, I love you so much," or "Jim, I'm so proud of you." The first name is important in lovemaking because our first names are embedded at the deepest level of our earliest memories.

- Focus together on a third object that's exciting, novel, beautiful, or interesting for the purpose of generating a mutually amplified positive moment.

- Find something that excites you personally and convert it for mutual use. Say you're having fun with your new purchase. Instead of expecting your partner to be as excited as you are, express your pleasure in a way that your partner can experience, such as "I'm so lucky to have you in my life."

Quiet, Loving, Relaxed States

A softer, more stable love experience is called *quiet love*. It's an arousal state that's both quiet and alert, associated with, among other things, lots of serotonin in the brain and body. Quiet love is important as it's a state consistent with absolute safety, security, and satisfaction (which is present in all secure-functioning relationships). Quiet love is closely related to gratitude, happiness, and contentment. Many couples are unable to cogenerate this state, but this is also something you and your partner can learn. The ability to generate quiet, loving, relaxed-alert states engenders feelings of safety and well-being.

Co-managing Distress

It's important to quickly and effectively co-manage distress. Distress states that are too intense or last too long (including repetition) will go into long-term memory. An increased sense of threat will accumulate and eventually alter the biology of both you and your partner.

If unabated, this process can and will take on a life of its own and threaten or destroy your relationship's safety and security system. Sounds terrible, I know. Yet this is very important for the two of you to deal with sooner rather than later. If you're in distress too much of the time, the bad feelings you accrue begin to mitigate the good ones. Over time, your physiology will orient toward a stress reaction every time you see or hear each other.

If you hurt your partner in some way, they may feel sad, angry, scared, ashamed, or a combination of these feelings. If you then disregard your partner's experience, dismiss it, or otherwise fail to repair the error, injustice, or misunderstanding, your partner will start to experience threat. If your partner doesn't recover in a timely manner from depression or rage, or continues to hurt you in the same manner, you will also experience threat. Threat isn't just physical. It can be a dangerous word (*ugly*), a phrase ("I can't do this anymore"), a face (raised chin and contemptuous expression), a voice or vocal sound (raised voice or expression of impatience), gestures or movements (finger pointing, arms folded), or a simple action such as turning that's seen as dismissive or rejecting. Threat is psychobiological in that it involves both the brain and body. (See chapter 9 on learning to fight well.)

Your Past Plays a Part

The experience of threat is highly subjective and memory based. So before you start accusing your partner of acting badly, remember that you're probably coming off similarly to your partner, and your partner is in all likelihood doing this without ill intent. If you determine that your partner is purposely, intentionally, actively behaving in a threatening manner, end the relationship NOW. But if you and your partner are like the vast majority of humans on this planet, you aren't intentionally threatening each other. That said, it's important to keep in mind that if you or your partner suffers from unresolved trauma or loss, the experience of threat may be more acute and chronic because there are more possible threat cues to grab your attention and convince you that the danger is real. If you or your partner suffers from unresolved trauma or loss, consider therapy with someone who specializes in couple work and trauma.

How do you know if you or your partner has *significant* unresolved trauma or loss? The answer is tricky. Many people carry around pockets of unresolved experience. For the most part, that shouldn't pose a problem except that it may come as a surprise to both of you if it pops up. We all have experienced pain or loss whereby we didn't get a lot of support, but those experiences didn't change our brain to the degree that we see danger all over the place. However, some of us were exposed to severe, continuous abuse and/or neglect early in childhood and never received any corrective experience to help us digest and integrate those experiences (see chapter 5). Like all living organisms, we adapted in order to survive. However, those adaptations could present as paranoia, given to rapid hyperarousal or hypoarousal, poor recovery from distress states, frequent dissociative episodes, extreme fearful reactions to novel situations, continuous vigilance, frequent bouts of collapse, bouts of significant disorientation, fearful reactions to touch or eye contact, fearful reactions to partner approach or withdrawal, derealization, and depersonalization.

Please don't start diagnosing yourself or your partner with the information I've provided. If you do suspect trauma, for yourself or your partner, seek professional support. Today many modalities can help people work through buried trauma, no matter how far back it goes.

Interpersonal Stress

Interpersonal stress is as it sounds: the kind of stress we encounter and endure when dealing with other people, especially our most important persons. Some people experience more acute and continuous interpersonal stress than others. A lot of this is due to negative childhood experiences where there was some measure of abuse or neglect. Love relationships are the hardest on the planet for a reason. For one, they refer back to the earliest relationships that carry both deeply positive and negative memories of dependency. For another, the expectations that are built into the adult romantic relationship are far and away unlike that of any other relationship, including parent-child.

Begin to pay attention to how well you and your partner manage distress. When assessing how good the two of you are at coregulation, notice *when* you make your observations. Are you both in a great, loving mood? If so, that could affect your assessment, as your state affects your memory. Similarly, if you make your observation in the middle of a fight, you will likely bias your assessment with memories of bad experiences.

Now that you know the ways in which your brain's negative bias affects you and your relationship, especially when in distress, it's important to also understand other factors that play into misunderstandings. In the next chapter, we will cover how memory, perception, and communication can be terribly flawed and create conflict and misperceptions, especially in your most important relationships.

4

THE TROUBLESOME TRIAD

Memory, Perception, and Communication

There are three main areas that cause conflict in relationships. I call them the *troublesome triad*—memory, perception, and communication. These areas can cause a couple to spiral into disconnection and fighting, and can undermine your couple bubble. This triad is often at the heart of both misunderstanding and threat escalation between partners. So how can we train ourselves in the areas of memory, perception, and communication so that these problem areas don't derail what has the potential to be a rich, life-enhancing marriage? It starts with some basic knowledge.

For some time, research has warned us that our memories are unreliable, and most of us don't understand how memory works. We fail to recognize that memory changes according to our current state of mind and therefore is misleading. Perception is yet another area of confusion unless one understands how perception is constantly being altered by both state of mind and memory. And believe it or not, verbal communication is almost always terrible; we mostly misunderstand each other. This gets compounded when what we say conflicts with our facial expressions and body language.

The point of this chapter is to understand not only yourself but all human beings—and to cut yourself and your partner a little slack. If you remember *anything* from this book, remember these three strictly human problem areas.

MEMORY

Memory is rarely laid down in a contiguous fashion. It's not like pressing record on your video camera. Not only is the record button in your brain not always on, but how you capture this information determines how it's played back in your mind. You fill in the gaps with made-up stuff—colors, emotions, and other confabulated and embellished data.

AN IMPORTANT FORMULA

State drives memory, memory drives state, and state alters perception. As you have an experience, you capture information through a variety of sense gateways such as vision, sound, smell, taste, and touch, as well as other sensations such as temperature. How you capture this information varies according to how much sleep you have had and other factors, including your current mental and emotional state.

As I start to feel bad about myself, I remember what I have to feel bad about. I start to notice people avoiding eye contact with me or not smiling and voilà—a totally false assumption comes together as true! Keep this in mind: You have never lived outside of your head—none of us have and never will. So it's not "all in your head" but rather "mostly all in your head."

Another problem is retrieval. Memory is encoded in a variety of ways: verbal, emotional, contextual, somatic (body experience), and so on. If you're paying attention, the experience you capture goes into short-term memory, which doesn't last very long. Therefore, how you record or encode the experience also determines how long it stays in memory. If that experience has lots of emotion to it or is unusual, it's likely to go from short-term to long-term memory. Emotion, or state of mind, affects memory by changing it. In just a bit I will explain why the opposite is also true: memory will affect emotion and state of mind.

Say you have an experience that's captured in memory. It's already different from the actual experience because it contains confabulations and embellishments. Now, when you practice re-memory, you change the memory based on how you feel in the moment. This is compounded because your "remembering" alters memory with each retelling. Here's the thing: our memory is closely connected to our sense of self, which is why losing our memory affects who we think we are. When someone challenges your memory, it can feel as if they're challenging who you are, which is why some couples are willing to fight "to the death." Can you see how easy it would be to argue about a shared experience? Once you have a deeper understanding of how memory works, you may not be so insistent that you're right.

When we get upset—and I mean really aroused, such as when we feel threatened—that record button in our brain stops working properly. The hippocampus, a part of our limbic system located in both sides of the temporal lobe, is mostly responsible for this as well as for short-term memory, which records experience based on place, context, and sequence. Without our hippocampus, we can't form new memories, find things, or put experiences into sequence and context.

This same thing happened to Barney and Betty.

Barney Last week, at Fred and Wilma's house, Fred told Pebbles and Bamm-Bamm that I wasn't coming to the Christmas party even though you and I hadn't talked about it yet. I'm really mad.

Betty Wait a second. That wasn't last week. And it wasn't at Fred and Wilma's house. You're talking about what happened two weeks ago at Pebbles's engagement party. Fred and Wilma were there.

Barney You've got it all wrong. I didn't go to Pebbles's engagement party because I was with Bamm-Bamm.

Betty You're such an idiot! I told you. You have attention deficit disorder. You can't even remember where you left your club.

This kind of exchange is typical. Betty and Barney likely experienced an event where they were emotionally overwhelmed. Neither encoded the experience exactly as it happened but rather from their own completely objective point of view, and thus they're unable to accurately sequence and contextualize the experience. Plus, they're both confused about where this occurred. What would be the solution to such a problem? Betty and Barney would be better off if they gave up trying to win the argument over whose memory is correct. Instead, they could just fix the misunderstanding and any hurt feelings and move on.

> **Barney** Maybe you're right. Who knows? I just hate it when you don't check with me before making plans.
>
> **Betty** You're right. I should have done that. I'm sorry, honey.

Done.

Our memory isn't what we think it is, and both people in a partnership need to own this truth. It's not worth fighting over unless you're trying to remember where you buried the treasure. Otherwise you're fighting over something that's outside your control, impersonal, unintentional, and simply part of the fallibility of the human brain.

PERCEPTION

Perception is like a funhouse mirror. It isn't at all what you think. Your perceptions are constantly being altered by your state of mind, which is being altered by your memory, and vice versa. What you think you hear may not actually be what you "hear." What you see may not actually be what you "see." The same with smell, taste, and touch—all of the senses will be altered by memory and arousal state.

Terry had a bad day at work. She came home and saw Paul relaxing on the couch. As she put her things down she asked Paul if he had fed the cat and changed the kitty litter. Paul lazily responded, "Of course." Terry had caught a glance of Paul's expression and took umbrage immediately.

Terry	Why the attitude?
Paul	What do you mean? What attitude? I said yes.
Terry	You said it with a mean tone and you looked angry.
Paul	No, I didn't!

Of course, Paul can't possibly know what his face looked like or what his voice sounded like. However, let's imagine that his face was neutral and his tone was without "attitude." If that's true, then what did Terry hear and see? She was already primed by her state of mind after a day in the office dealing with some difficult employees, one of whom had a very bad attitude. People were angry with her, and she with them. When she entered her home and saw Paul lounging on the couch, her brain was already primed, and so she *saw* an angry face and *heard* a negative tone of voice. She trusted her perceptions. We make these kinds of mistakes more than we realize, but that's not the problem. It's that we unequivocally *believe* our perceptions and memories.

COMMUNICATION

As a teacher and therapist, I get into lots of trouble with language. It's not so much that I misuse it, at least not intentionally, but rather that words mean different things to different people. For example, when I introduce the term *couple bubble* or the phrase *managing your partner*, my students will challenge my word choice, even suggesting that I use dangerous words and phrases—something entirely different from my meaning. I used to feel frustrated, even ashamed, that my words were taken out of context or interpreted as hurtful. But I understand that misinterpreting language is a universal problem.

It reminds me of principles of speaking and listening, such as those put forth by British philosopher of language Paul Grice and Princeton professor and psychologist George Miller. Grice's maxim suggests the speaker be collaborative and coherent with the listener by remaining concise, to the point, relevant, and truthful. In all cases the speaker should make it easy for the listener to follow. Miller's law concerns the listener, who should assume that what the speaker is saying is true and must work to determine what the speaker means to convey. Ah, if we all practiced these rules of speech and listening. But we don't. We don't have time. We also believe we're being clear, heard, and understood. And that hardly happens. Even when we're listening, we're misunderstanding the speaker to a large extent. It's not all due to laziness or inattentiveness.

Since we *are* what we know and what we've experienced, new information will naturally be incorporated into our current framework. When attempting to learn something new, I'm going to understand it within the context of what I already know. This process is called *assimilation*, a term popularized by cognitive theorist Jean Piaget. It's far easier to integrate new knowledge than its cognitive cousin, *accommodation*, a process whereby I must fundamentally change my way of thinking about new information in order to understand it. The latter always causes more distress and confusion. When discussing ideas or personal perspectives with one another, we naturally attempt to understand what the other means through our own lens. This may sound too obvious a notion, yet the amount of effort needed to interpret what's true is often too much for partners, so it's as if they're talking in different languages to each other. It's hard to understand something outside of our personal experience and knowledge. It's even more effortful when we *need* to understand and be understood.

When you go to another country where you don't speak the language, you rely on a kind of sign language. Believe it or not, you will communicate much better that way than when you begin to understand the language even a little bit. Once you have some understanding of the language, you know enough to be dangerous. Instead of trying to communicate nonverbally, you attempt to use new words and phrases, which can get you into a lot of trouble, and not because you're not familiar with the language. If only that were the truth. Even speaking your own language will get you into trouble, because words and phrases have different meanings to different people. You may think you're being clear with another person. They may *think* they understand what you're saying. But that's an illusion. Remember, real time is very fast. Our brain is mostly automatic; it matches things up instantaneously with our memory using shortcuts. What could possibly go wrong? Everything.

Free Audio Programs!

The Self-Acceptance Project ($97 value)
Instant access to 23 respected spiritual teachers and more than 26 hours of transformational teachings on self-compassion, especially during challenging times.

The Practice of Mindfulness ($15 value)
Download guided practices by Jon Kabat-Zinn, Shinzen Young, Kelly McGonigal, Tara Brach, Sharon Salzberg, and Jack Kornfield.

Meditation Music ($10 value)
Listen to nine inspiring tracks for healing, relaxation, and releasing stress.

To download these **3 free gifts** go to **SoundsTrue.com/Free**

sounds true
many voices, one journey

800.333.9185

Dear **Sounds True friend,**

Since 1985, Sounds True has been sharing spiritual wisdom and resources to help people live more genuine, loving, and fulfilling lives. We hope that our programs inspire and uplift you, enabling you to bring forth your unique voice and talents for the benefit of us all.

We would like to invite you to become part of our growing online community by giving you three downloadable programs—an introduction to the treasure of authors and artists available at Sounds True! To receive these gifts, just flip this card over for details, then visit us at **SoundsTrue.com/Free** and enter your email for instant access.

With love on the journey,

TAMI SIMON   Founder and Publisher, Sounds True

SOUNDS TRUE
many voices, one journey   800.333.9185

Additionally, we only ever approximate each other's minds. It's likely that we're rarely, if ever, on the same page exactly, even when we think we understand each other. It's highly likely that any interaction is fraught with errors and misunderstandings. So why don't we complain more often? Because when we feel good about ourselves or each other, we fill in blanks with things that are positive; we make accommodations, we cut each other slack, and, more importantly, we think we understand. But when we don't feel very good about ourselves or each other, our memories and perceptions change, and the communication mistakes can radically increase. So many times I see partners arguing about two different things without even knowing it. That's how easy it is for communication to go off the rails.

Here's an example.

Brad and Amy are getting ready for bed. They have a ritual where they watch a TV show every night, and tonight, for Amy at least, is no different. Brad, on the other hand, is overly tired and is signaling that he wants to be asleep. His eyes are closed, and his hands and arms are at his sides.

> **Amy** [tickling Brad's body, trying to get his attention]
> Let's watch our show.
>
> **Brad** [smiling and giggling because of Amy's tickling]
> Mmm. Um. Hmm.
>
> **Amy** Come on! I'm ready to watch the show.
>
> **Brad** Honey, I'm so tired.
>
> **Amy** This will wake you up.
>
> **Brad** [continues to make moaning sounds]
>
> **Amy** Come on. I'm turning it on. [Amy gets up out of bed to turn on the TV.]
>
> **Brad** Sweetheart, I really want to go to sleep.
>
> **Amy** [makes an exaggerated sad face] But we always watch the show together.
>
> **Brad** You can watch it alone tonight. It's okay.
> [There's a long silence. Brad's eyes are closed. Amy is sitting up with her upper lip tucked into her lower lip, thinking and staring at Brad.]

Amy	Okay. Go to sleep. [short pause] Could you turn off the light?
Brad	[He doesn't respond except for a muted moan.]
Amy	Turn off the light.
Brad	Honey, I'm trying to fall asleep. You turn off the light.
Amy	But it's right next to you.
Brad	No, it's not! Come on, honey. If you want it off, turn it off yourself. [Brad turns his back to Amy and tries to sleep.]

Amy sits there fuming. She believes Brad is punishing her. As Brad lies on his side, he thinks Amy is punishing him for not watching TV with her. In a couple of hours, she wakes up furious and hits Brad on the arm to wake him. This event gains momentum, creating a downward spiral. Neither Brad nor Amy say goodbye to the other as they leave for work in the morning, and they're left to deal with the hurt and resentment that following evening.

Now here's what actually happened. Brad, who tends to avoid conflict, has a hard time telling Amy that he wants to sleep and not watch TV. Fearing she will be unhappy with this boundary, he pretends to go to sleep while smiling as she tickles him. His reaction sends a confusing message to Amy. Instead of letting her know he's too tired to watch TV, he gives her the impression that he could be cajoled out of his sleepiness. He continues the charade until he's forced to tell her that he wants to sleep. Keeping his eyes closed and not looking at her has a dismissive effect on Amy, who doesn't like to feel blown off. Though disappointed, Amy feels threatened by Brad's body stiffness and closed eyes. (Note the body language.) Rather than talk about this, she simply says "Okay" and withdraws. Brad then turns his back to Amy, further making her feel disregarded, dismissed, and abandoned. Amy's annoyance begins to escalate inside. Now she wants the light turned off. Believing that Brad is actually closest to the light switch, she asks him to turn it off, thinking it's the least he could do. Brad, upon hearing this request, believes Amy is angry with him and is passive-aggressively expecting him to turn off the light even after he has "showed" her that he's tired. Brad is thinking, "How inconsiderate. Amy is trying to punish me again." Feeling angry himself, Brad has a hard time falling asleep and instead rehearses in his mind all the things he'd like to say to Amy but dares not express them. As she watches the TV show, the light still on, Amy has her own angry thoughts. "What an asshole. His unwillingness to turn off the light is confirmation that he's distancing from me."

If one were to look back, one would see that Brad has a history of feeling intruded upon by his mother. He's very sensitive to demands being made on him. Amy has a history of being abandoned and ignored by her father. Both are reliving those experiences, and both are reenacting their worst fears from their family histories. It's no surprise when everything comes to a head and one of them explodes.

GIVING AND RECEIVING CUES AND CLUES

When it comes to communication, we give and receive many signals that are nonverbal, such as our facial expressions and body language. These cue our partner as to how we feel when they're talking. These signals also give us clues about when it's our turn to provide verbal feedback. This is called the *signal-response system*. In a very important way, the signal-response system is what makes or breaks secure attachment and a secure-functioning relationship. It affects both attachment security and arousal regulation in significant ways.

The signal-response system is first experienced during infancy, when the baby signals nonverbally to the caregiver—for example, the mother. The baby might coo or smile, and the mother responds and signals back by smiling and cooing or talking baby talk to which her baby responds, and so on. This back-and-forth between them is called the *signal-response stream*, and it's rife with errors. Think of it as two separate minds trying to find each other; only in this instance, the responsibility is placed squarely on the mother. In the case of a crying baby, the mother must connect with the baby again and again to understand what she needs. She might try picking her up, feeding her, changing a wet diaper, and so on, until she reads the signal correctly. This requires a caregiver with the energy and curiosity to "locate the baby's mind" over and over again. This interactive function is called *interactive regulation* (caregiver-baby-caregiver) but it begins with external regulation (caregiver to baby). In order for the caregiver to find the baby, they must allow the baby to lead much of the time. If the caregiver insists on leading, they will only find themselves.

The signal-response system is very fast and has granular components that are almost microscopic and largely faster than thought. All of these interactions are seemingly fluid until they're not. Errors or glitches go unnoticed because these two nervous systems will automatically error-correct swiftly. However, if a series of errors repeat (a cluster of micromoments) or sustain, or if swift error correction isn't forthcoming (a matter of milliseconds), then a subjective experience of distress will arise. This distress often appears first as anxiety, yet it can escalate rapidly and become frustration, fear, anger, and eventually threat.

When a baby signals and the response takes too long, the baby's level of distress increases and becomes part of the calculus for future signaling. Failure to respond to the baby's signals definitely has consequences. If the baby signals but the caregiver responds incorrectly, this too becomes part of the infant's future signaling calculus. If the baby suffers a consequence for having signaled in the first place—perhaps the caregiver responds in a hostile manner—this affects how the baby will signal in the future.

Now, don't read this and freak out that you're a terrible parent or that your parents were evil. We're talking here about consistent patterns of signal-response disturbance. There's no interaction without error. There's only consistent failure to error-correct, reattune, or repair the infraction. When sustained or repeated signal-response events occur within a couple, partners become dysregulated (out of sorts). These errors are commonly called misattuned micromoments, where partners are out of tune with each other.

Poor Signaling Is Experienced Differently

People with a history of secure attachment (secures) generally have less problems embedded in the signal-response system than do those with a history of insecure attachment (insecures). (More on this in chapter 5.) Secures have plenty of bodily memories of being responded to appropriately and without consequence. Not generally so with insecures. Think of the baby who was ignored or yelled at for crying when they were hungry. Although secures generally signal appropriately, they too can either be over- or underexpressive, depending on many factors, not all of which are attachment related. Same with responsiveness. Generally speaking, secures aren't as sensitive to errors in the signal-response system, though they may complain of problems in that area with their partner. Errors are errors, and over- or underresponsiveness can go too far with anyone, secure or insecure. However, insecures, due to their early histories, can be especially reactive to signal-response issues.

Insecure avoidant individuals tend to be low signalers and poor responders. This is likely due to having had at least one primary caregiver who underresponded and undersignaled. This underresponse can also manifest in low expression in the lower, middle, or upper parts of the face, making them harder to read. Low expression can also be observed in tone of voice and body posture. Avoidant folks tend to use more facial controls than do secures. This may be due to being exposed to facial controls in their family of origin or to the predilection for protecting themselves from intrusion. The face is our social organ, and we use it, especially close up, to read what's going on inside our partner's mind. If a person is sensitive to exposure, it makes sense that they would want to control portions of their face in order to protect themselves from showing difficult emotions, such as shame.

But controls can also be used to mask what someone is really feeling or thinking, making the face appear deceptive. Sometimes controls include providing an outward expression that's quite different from how someone feels inside. Their smile can hide angry feelings, tears may be a substitute for anger, and contempt can replace sadness. This gets trickier if there's a strong reflexive defense against attack or exposure to vulnerability. For instance, some will underrespond due to fear because they learned to stay still lest the caregiver becomes angrier, more threatening—or worse—unpredictable. It's a form of self-protection. However, these defenses can be misinterpreted, wherein those with low signaling are seen as disinterested, unfriendly, or even threatening. Many studies have examined faces that remain too still and, as a result, can produce a threat response in both babies and adults.[1]

Some insecures tend to oversignal both verbally and nonverbally. They also tend to be the recipients of overresponse to their signals and may be the ones who experienced consequences for signaling when they were young, such as the caregiver's frustration. Likewise, many adult partners have admitted to signaling more loudly or dramatically in childhood in order to get a response. Because they tend to overexpress facially and vocally, they appear to some as dramatic or histrionic. These partners may be particularly sensitive to those who underrespond and exhibit low signaling. Due to their fears of withdrawal and abandonment, these particular insecures can become very anxious and agitated if they don't receive enough feedback from their partner.

Poor Signaling Affects Arousal Regulation

As you have learned, in a two-person system, the autonomic and central nervous systems are linked and regulated by each partner. Each partner will respond to internal and external stimuli differently based on their childhood experiences with signaling and responding. Even the most secure-functioning couples will struggle from time to time around signal-response issues.

Mitch and Kendall, who frequently get into trouble when discussing topics important to one or both of them, are a good example of a couple who struggle with signal-response issues. Here's some background: Mitch was raised by a cold, distant, and judgmental mother who didn't respond if he was upset. Kendall was raised by a ranting father who lectured her and "loved to hear himself talk." She wouldn't dare interrupt her father when she was little. In fact, she remembers sitting there wishing he'd just go away and leave her alone. When discussing a problem, Mitch expresses himself in an animated, emotional manner, and Kendall will sit quietly, poised, and almost perfectly still while Mitch speaks. He appears to talk without pause and becomes increasingly repetitive and excited (aroused). Kendall's expressions remain the same—unflinching, imperturbable, but present. It's no surprise when their conversations lead to distress.

Why does Mitch go on and on like that? Why does Kendall allow him to do that? Relatively unaware of himself, Mitch is largely reacting to Kendall's unresponsiveness, believing she doesn't understand him or is judging him. He's not altogether wrong. Kendall is indeed waiting for him to finish, which he doesn't do because she's not signaling a need to talk, nor is she responding to his nonverbal cues. Kendall's lack of facial expression causes Mitch to believe she is thinking something negative and he feels judged, like when his mother judged him. Kendall's and Mitch's fighting styles are actually amplifying their personal historical traumas, yet neither is aware.

So how can they remedy the situation? One option is for Mitch to pay attention to Kendall's subtle cues while talking, which includes stillness, and checking in with her. Another is for Kendall to offer a response by nodding her head or saying phrases such as "I see," "I understand," or even "Okay, uh-huh." She can also use touch and eye contact to stop him from repeating himself: "Honey, hold on. I get it. You're wanting me to . . . " And if he continues to talk too long, she can say, "One more minute and let's change the subject," as a way to take control of the subject matter without hurting Mitch's feelings.

The troublesome triad, if not understood as a problem intrinsic to the human condition, will lead to countless misunderstandings that you and your partner will presume to be intentional and personal. Therefore, can you fully trust your communication? Nope. Can you fully trust your memories? Nope. Can you fully trust your perceptions? Nope. So what can you trust? As my colleague Cary Glass has taught repeatedly to our medical residents, be curious, not furious. Check and cross-check your perceptions: what you hear, what you say, and what your partner hears. Ask yourself: Are we talking about the same thing? Is my face saying something different from my words? Is my voice? Is the shortcut I'm using with my partner really being understood?

All of us can become arrogant about what we believe is true. The best way to error-correct is to remain curious, friendly, flexible, humble, and open to being wrong. Your relationship's integrity is what keeps you safe and secure, not your adherence to fact, righteousness, performance, or perfection.

5

WHAT ARE YOUR STYLES
OF RELATING?

Most of us would like a jump-start toward understanding more about ourselves and our romantic partner. We go to therapy, read self-help books, go to spiritual advisors, and consult personality and compatibility tests. There are many ways of investigating personality, including the Keirsey Temperament Sorter or the Myers-Briggs Type Indicator, although both are more commonly used by employers, not lovers.

While these personality tests are interesting and often helpful, there's another avenue of insights into styles of relating from an attachment point of view. While all the other typing systems help us gain insight into one another and how to work together, it's primarily an understanding of how we relate—our attachment style—that will set us up for success in terms of a healthy, long-term partnership. Attachment styles determine how we connect, how we fight, and whether we value our self or our relationships first.

WE RELATE BASED ON ATTACHMENT STYLE

Attachment theory is a psychological model of interpersonal relationships that begins at birth and continues throughout the lifespan. It became a focus of attention in the 1950s in the United Kingdom by John Bowlby,[1] James Robinson, and others,[2] and in the United

States by Harry Harlow, who famously studied rhesus monkeys.[3] The study of monkey attachment bridged an important discovery in all primates, including human children and adults. Through these studies researchers learned that attachment bonds with other human beings are fundamental to human survival. We need to feel connected to at least one other person and that need for connection is both psychological and biological.

Attachment begins with our earliest caregiver, often referred to as the *primary attachment figure*. While there may be other attachment figures and caregivers, there's always a primary person, usually the mother. Attachment isn't simply about Mother but rather relationships with very important others, particularly those upon whom you depended when you were young—mother, father, siblings, teachers, friends, religious figures, and so on. That humans attach to other humans is pretty much a given. However, it's the *quality* of the attachment that we're going to discuss in this chapter.

Let's take the mother as an example of the earliest primary attachment figure.

MOTHER-BLAMING

Allow me to say something about how the field of psychology has cast mothers. When teaching attachment to my students, I have a slide on my PowerPoint with a subtitle that's supposed to be a joke: "If it's not one thing, it's your mother." We've blamed mothers for a very long time. From the 1950s to 1970s, it was the *schizophrenogenic mother*, coined in 1948 by Frieda Fromm-Reichmann, whereby the mother could be blamed for inducing schizophrenia in her offspring. The term *refrigerator mother* was coined in the 1950s, pointing the finger at a cold maternal figure as the cause of autism. There are helicopter mothers, tiger moms, free-range moms, and crunchy moms. Mother-blaming has been around for a long time (thanks, Sigmund) and a new feminist psychological movement is pushing back. Today, mothers are damned if they stay at home or if they work. It's enough that mothers (and fathers) worry themselves sick over messing up their kids, without having to read what experts have to say about how they messed up their kids.

Bonding begins in utero with the fetus becoming accustomed to the mother's heartbeat and voice. After birth, the totally dependent infant continues to bond to the mother's voice, smell, taste, and touch. A kind of imprinting takes place as mother and baby remain in a singular orbit of nonverbal face-to-face, skin-to-skin, and nervous system–to–nervous system interaction. The baby is continually adapting and changing according to both internal and external events. The quality of attachment the baby experiences—meaning how much contact the baby gets and whether that contact is stressful or calm—determines the baby's ability to develop naturally.

Secure attachment means that the infant or child is confident that their primary caregiver(s) will appropriately respond to their needs and communicate in a timely fashion (which is subjective according to the child's developmental grasp of time). An insecure attachment means the child is either unsure or is certain that their primary caregiver(s) will either be unresponsive, inappropriately responsive, or perhaps punitive in response to the child's attempt to signal distress. Consider this formula: infant/child signals, caregiver responds (time it takes and appropriateness), and there's a consequence for having signaled the caregiver.

In other words, if the attachment to the mother is secure—meaning the baby knows their needs for love, nourishment, and nurturing will be met—the infant's internal resources are relaxed and primed for growth and development. However, if the attachment relationship is insecure—meaning the baby fears that their physical and emotional needs aren't the primary concern of their caregivers—the infant's resources are compromised and therefore growth and development may also be compromised.

For instance, if the mother is depressed, she might be unable to provide the continuous attention the baby requires. Since the baby's survival rests in the primary's ability to be mostly present and available, internal resources may be unnecessarily tied up by the infant's uncertainty.

Secure attachment is facilitated by caregivers who are consistently available, fully resourced, sensitive, interested, and focused on the baby's nonverbal communication. As the baby develops, the criteria for safety and security continues to expand. A toddler, for instance, requires attention and presence from the primary caregiver, but also needs the caregiver to provide a more complex understanding and precise sensitivity to their internal world. This need for complexity and sensitivity continues as the child develops and receives multiple neurobiological upgrades on their way to adulthood.

A secure infant, child, teenager, and adult feels confident in their connection to loved ones without fear of abandonment or engulfment. The secure child is free to move away from and return to the primary's field of near vision, without negative consequences, while the caregiver remains fully attentive and present. As a child goes through developmental challenges that increase the child's distress, negativity, and ambivalence, the secure caregiver absorbs the child's negativism without overreaction and punishment. In other words, the secure caregiver is developmentally capable of self-regulation (keeping their cool) when in the presence of a dysregulated child, remaining neither threatened by the child's need for autonomy nor their need for dependency. This caregiver can accurately interpret the child's internal world while remaining curious and ready to error-correct or repair mistakes or injuries. So secure attachment is the result of a deeply relationship-centered value system in which relationship integrity is of central importance, whereas insecure attachment is the result of a self-centered value system where an individual's need is of greater importance.

Studies on attachment cross-culturally look at two types of societies: individualistic and collectivistic. Western cultures (United States, Britain, and Europe) tend to be individualist-centered while Eastern cultures (China, Japan, and Israel) are more collectivist. It may be that attachment is simply too Western to be accurately applied to other societies. That said, Western studies appear to confirm repeatedly that child and adult attachment affect close relationships throughout life. Attachment isn't static and unchangeable. We shift and change in our attachment security as we mature and grow in relationships with important others.

ARE YOU AN ISLAND, A WAVE, OR AN ANCHOR?

You can think of attachment styles as you would a culture. You go to another country and the people there do things differently. You must learn the culture to get along and to understand the meaning of what people do. For example, go to Japan and you will find that people there bow instead of shaking hands. Eye contact is perceived differently in Japan than it is in the United States. In Japan people often avert their gaze, not because they're ashamed or trying to ignore the other person but rather out of deference. Looking in your teacher's eyes in many Asian countries is seen as utter disrespect, whereas not making eye content with a teacher in the United States would be considered disrespectful.

Families have cultures too. Family styles that appreciate attachment values tend to be more relationship focused, more affectionate, warmer, and supportive. Family styles that focus more on the self, performance levels, appearances, and/or independence tend to be less affectionate, with a colder relating style. In family variations where children are expected to take care of their parents—one or both parents may be disabled, depressed, mentally ill, or addicted to drugs or alcohol—there may be warmth and affection but there's also an over-emphasis on remaining dependent.

Also consider that your caregivers were quite different from one another. One may have been very warm and the other quite cold. One valued relationships more than the other. One valued independence while the other dependence. One caregiver required support for their self-esteem while the other required nothing. We often take on the "style" of the closest parent before the age of twelve. To which parent were you the closest and at what age? With whom did you spend the most time and at what age? Were you your father's favorite? You mother's? Neither? Were you raised by someone other than your mother or father? What was the quality of that relationship and at what age?

We can assume one of three main states (intermittent) or traits (constant) when relating to others—that of the island, the wave, or the anchor, and each is its own culture. The *anchor* is the most secure. Anchors are relatively undisturbed by fears of abandonment or engulfment by partners. They're relatively unencumbered by concerns of moving toward and away from important others. They enjoy seeking physical and emotional proximity with their primary attachment partners. They enjoy maintaining physical and emotional contact, without experiencing distress. They adapt easily to change, maintain investment in tasks and people during periods of frustration, and maintain healthy self-entitlements with regard to career, professional development, personal development, successful relationships with others, appropriate and reciprocal relationships with lovers, maintenance of good health, and so on. They get along with a wide range of personalities with varied interests and are skilled socially and emotionally. Anchors easily access their emotions and are expressive with others. They have very good control over their impulses and desires and play well with others. People like being around anchors because they're less emotionally complicated; they're easier, better humored, happier, and better adjusted than deeply rooted islands and waves. Anchors are neither aggressive nor wimpy. They're accustomed to cooperating and collaborating with others. For them, secure functioning in a love relationship comes easily and naturally.

In contrast, you have the *island* and the *wave*, both relatively insecure when in close, committed love relationships. Please remember that *insecures*—a term used to refer to the entire group—have several things in common, the most central being their bottom-line focus on self over relationship. Islands and waves operate as one-person psychological systems of "me first." Both come from early interactions that were unfair, unjust, and insensitive too much of the time. Think of islands as more distancing and waves as more clinging, although at times both are clinging and distancing. Islands pride themselves in being independent and self-reliant. They tend to be more sensitive to feelings of intrusion, engulfment, interference, and exploitation (being used). They're the do-it-yourself people and need more alone time than others. They experience more interpersonal stress during sustained interactions with others than any other group. This explains why they can seem cool or distant emotionally and physically.

The wave's ambivalence about dependency can bring about rapid shifts between clinging and distancing. Unlike islands, waves tend to be warmer and more emotionally expressive. They're more likely to seek closeness and desire maintaining physical and emotional contact over longer periods. Their emotions tend to go up and down, often as a result of their external environment. Unlike islands who need alone time to process, waves need to talk through their problems in order to calm their nervous systems. Waves value interaction with others, both through verbal interaction and physical closeness.

The Island

Now that you know a little about the three main states we can assume when relating, let's examine the island in more detail. I refer to this as the distancing family culture. In the psychological literature on attachment these people are called avoidant, anxious avoidant, dismissive, or derogating of attachment values, but I prefer the friendlier term *island*. As I mentioned before, islands tend to put self needs ahead of relationship values.

Making an Island

Self-esteem and social standing are important to island parents. There's an implicit or explicit expectation that island children perform well in all things and/or appear well to the outside world, because it reflects well on the family. Other values such as money, intelligence, power, beauty, and youth may also be at play. Island parents discourage dependency and neediness. These parents are typically less affectionate and less expressive than wave or anchor parents. They often expect their children to support one or both parents' sense of self, or at least never challenge it. Island parents tend to be secretive, withholding, difficult to approach, intolerant of conflict and challenge, dismissive, withdrawn, and critical of others. Shame usually plays a big role in the island world. Because self-esteem is always an issue and failure is often experienced as shameful, shame is one of the prevailing emotions that's unregulated on this island.

Because dependency is discouraged, island parents often expect their children to take care of themselves and play by themselves quietly. In the American culture, a well-behaved child is one who plays quietly alone, never cries, is never fussy, and is basically easy. However, many of these children are mistaken for anchors when they're really islands (see below). Studies have shown that island babies and children are more anxious than even those from the clinging group. The stress is evidenced by corticosteroid-related hormones and neurotransmitters in the brain, blood, and urine of island children.

How Islands Interact with Others

All human beings signal to a primary person for response of some kind. Babies signal to be fed, burped, or held, or to have their diapers changed. The signals are, of course, nonverbal (in the talking sense). For the baby to feel safe and secure, the response should be relatively swift and attuned to the signaled need. The degree to which the caregiver doesn't respond in a timely fashion or provides the wrong response will affect whether the child's future signaling is either amplified or muted. For instance, if a baby or child signals and either gets no response or the wrong response repeatedly, or experiences negative consequences for having signaled in the first place, that will become the calculus by which the child signals in the future.

Island children tend to be low expressive and low contact depending on their parents' ability to express a full range of emotions and to value physical affection. Island children are taught early on that their needs may not be tended to promptly, so they tend to signal (for help or attention) far less than other children. We might call them low signal. Because of their tendency to play alone, island children often immerse themselves in fantasy.

How Islands Restore Internal Peace and Balance

Part of human development is learning to manage our emotional and physiological states. Islands use, sometimes singularly, a self-management style called *autoregulation* to bring them back to a calm state. Autoregulation is one of four strategies of self-care, all of which are normal and natural. Think self-soothe and self-stimulate, without the need of another person. Islands will remove themselves from stressful situations, staying by themselves until they can "get it together." While this works great for them—remember, they adapted as children to manage themselves—anchor and wave partners will take offense at their withdrawal. When autoregulation is overused as a strategy, others can feel ignored, unwanted, unloved, rejected, or abandoned.

Autoregulation is an energy-conserved state that's closely linked to dissociation, stemming from overfocus. This could be confused with attention deficit disorder. Individuals who are overly reliant on autoregulation tend to have a hard time shifting from the dreamlike state of autoregulation to the more stressful interpersonal state of interaction. Since islands tend to autoregulate as a practice, these individuals will likely have trouble shifting from being alone to interacting with others, but won't have any difficulty shifting from interaction to being alone. It's like a door that swings in only one direction.

ISLAND STATE SHIFTING

From interaction to noninteraction = easy

From noninteraction to interaction = hard

Autoregulation affects focus and awareness. Have you ever had someone who was fully awake talk to you while you're just waking up? Your mind can't possibly follow the speed and the information that's coming at you. You may become confused and flooded, and you may find yourself feeling angry at the person talking to you. Islands tend to feel that way when interrupted while in the autoregulatory mode.

Islands Value Self over Relationships

There's another reason why autoregulators don't like to be intruded upon. The nature of the island perspective is to focus on self needs over relationship integrity. The island always assumes that the approaching person wants or needs something without reciprocity or mutuality. This long-held memory leads to a reflex that can be angry, dismissive, avoiding, or even attacking.

Because openness isn't exhibited in an island worldview, it's understandable that island children and island adults keep their cards close to their chests. They have secrets. They also tend to compartmentalize. Many of their secrets are shame-bound around sex or sexuality, but they may also focus on money, intelligence, power, beauty, and youth. Their secrets can involve one or many of these needs and can lead to betrayals involving not just sex but also money and other important decisions that would otherwise be made mutually. The secure individual would view keeping secrets as dishonest or noncollaborative; the island sees secrets as self-protective and necessary for survival. After all, important members of their family weren't forthcoming, honest, transparent, or collaborative. This isn't a personality defect. The island is simply behaving according to their cultural upbringing. Because the self is the central element in the island ethos, islands have great fear of losing themselves or their autonomy in a committed attachment relationship. Islands are also afraid of losing their things or belongings, which includes money.

As a therapist I've noticed that islands tend to use more controls to mask what could be going on inside. Because islands are shame-bound and secretive, they loathe to have people read them well. Islands also tend to use a lot of control on their face and body. At times, portions of their face will either not move or will move in a highly controlled manner. The lack of facial motility or spontaneous movement may have to do with the way members of their family of origin moved their faces. Controls are viewed as the effort used to manage, hold back, change, or hide internal reactions by tightening or controlling muscle movement. These controls tend to make islands appear more deceptive than others, as if they're hiding something.

Islands and Conflict

One of the hallmarks of islands is conflict avoidance and passive-aggressiveness. Islands avoid conflict unless backed against the wall. After a fight, the island wishes to just forget. In fact, forgetting is part of the island system. Islands tend to push away negative feelings such as sadness, depression, anger, and shame. If possible, they will dismiss or forget painful emotions. While good for them, this distancing defense is often experienced as threatening to most partners who prefer to engage and work through conflict. But the conflict-avoiding island will refuse to do this thereby creating a threat to their partner. One of the reasons islands avoid conflict is their fear that an attachment relationship is too fragile to handle the truth about them. They use the mechanism of avoidance because they fear being discovered and then rejected. One must forgive the island for this practice because their real past experiences have taught them that transparency leads to big trouble.

Island behavior doesn't represent abnormality or pathology. It's an adaptation to environment, something that was mandatory for surviving childhood. And islands don't recognize their behavior. If you lived in a fishbowl all your life, you would think it normal, having never lived in another environment. So as adults, islands don't have an inkling that their ways can cause problems in relationships with others who have different attachment styles. The defensive structure of the island assures the self that the problems lie outside. It's only through repeated offenses to the self, likely in the form of relationship distress or abandonment, that the island would begin to seek help.

Do you want to be with an island? Why not? If that island is personally aware and understands their reflexes that prevent a secure-functioning relationship, then by all means, take the island. If, on the other hand, you're with an island who's neither personally aware nor finds their island defenses destructive to self and other, then you should absolutely pass on this person.

I'm an Island

Me Tell me about yourself.

Her Boy, I was looked at as the also-ran. My younger sister was a star skier. In fact, she even went to the Olympics! I, on the other hand, was the responsible one. My brother, the youngest, got away with everything. I got away with nothing. I was my father's favorite, which is strange being that I'm a girl. He always had praise for me and only got mad if I got bad grades.

    Both my parents are overachievers—and that's saying it lightly. My mother graduated cum laude and is a high-level bureaucrat at the State Department. My father is a molecular biologist and a well-known professor at Stanford. I studied cell biology in grad school at Stanford also, and now work at the Centers for Disease Control in Washington, DC. My husband is a stay-at-home father. He was a Green Beret and now he's Colonel Mom. He doesn't complain about this, but I do. I have this work ethic, you know. I can't stand to see him hang around the house. Is that wrong? I mean, he *is* doing something and helping me with child-rearing.

    My parents have always been ambitious. I don't remember them doing much together except having occasional bridge parties at the house. We weren't really allowed downstairs with the adults. Occasionally my father would bring me and my sister out to brag about us. I liked it at the time, but now, when I think about it, it made me a little uncomfortable, as if we were brought out as show ponies, not unique individuals. We did a lot of bragging in my family. My father needed to feel special, and so did my mother, though she expressed it in a different way. She'd compare me to her when she was a kid, but I always came up short—never as smart or smarter. My little sister wasn't subjected to this because my mother had no athletic ability, so there was no comparison or competition with her. Because my parents were always so busy when I was a kid, we had housekeepers who made us breakfast and lunch.

Me When you were a child, who hugged you, held you, rocked you, kissed you?

Her My parents were not big on affection. In fact, I can't remember a time when either of my parents kissed or hugged me. Now, when I try to hug my mother, it's super awkward. And my father? Never!

Me When you were a child, which adult played with you—just you?

Her That would be nobody. We played with kids on the street if we played at all. We pretty much took care of ourselves as children.

Me When you got upset as a child, what would your parents do?

Her I don't remember getting upset. I was a good kid. No, I was a perfect kid. I never caused any trouble. I would get up in the morning, make my bed, go to school, stay at school and finish my work, come home, and do more homework. Many times, my parents were out during the night. My mother traveled for the State Department. My father would travel abroad to give talks. I rarely saw them travel together.

Me When you were a child, who put you to bed at night?

Her Nobody. We put ourselves to bed.

Me All kids get scared at night at a certain age. Do you remember getting scared at night?

Her Yeah, I would. I would just pull the covers over my head or go into my sister's room. She'd come into my room if she was scared also. Sometimes we would just goof around in our rooms together. Nobody would stop us. It felt as if we were doing something we weren't supposed to be doing, so it was fun. I miss those times with my sister. We don't talk anymore. We had a falling out some years ago when I married someone my parents didn't like. I guess I married outside of my "class." My husband isn't college educated. He's not somebody who can talk about the things my parents like to talk about. He's also unimpressed with my parents' boastfulness.

Me How do you feel about your husband?

Her Well, like I said, he's a great guy, and I love him. It does bother me that he's not interested in things that I'm interested in. I think the fact that he's unimpressed with my parents sometimes makes me feel as if maybe he's unimpressed with me. I'm used to impressing people, you know.

Me When you were a child, did your parents look like they were in love?

Her I guess that depends on what you mean by "in love." I mean, they're always civil to each other, but there was no real affection. I never saw them fight. They seemed to have their own separate lives. My husband complains that I'm not very warm. I think I'm a warm person, just not a touchy-feely sort. I like it sometimes, but other times it bugs me. But I would say that my husband and I are much more demonstrative than my parents behaved.

Me When you were a child and you were sick, who took care of you?

Her I don't remember getting sick. I suppose it was one of our housekeepers. I actually don't have a lot of memories. That's kind of strange to me.

Me So when you were sick, one of your housekeepers would bring you medicine?

Her Let me think for a moment. I think it was my mother who would take me to the doctor.

Me Yeah, but did she spend time with you at all when you were sick? Did she lie down with you, read to you, watch television with you?

Her No, never. I don't remember being sick much because I was always expected to go to school. If I was sick at home, I'm sure I was alone. Today if I get sick I don't like anybody fussing over me. It annoys me. I just like to be left alone. I like my alone time and I like my privacy. I also like my independence. My husband is pretty good about this, but every now and then he gets needy and that really triggers me. I'm not very good with neediness.

Me How do you and your husband handle fighting?

Her Fighting? We don't fight. At least I don't. I hate fighting. I hate any kind of conflict. I want to get out of it as quickly as possible or just not deal with it. I guess my way of dealing with conflict is to withdraw. My husband hates this with a passion. My thinking is, you just get over it. You move on. Life is too short. Focus on the important things.

The Wave

Now for the wave. Like ocean waves, they move in and pull back. Like islands, waves are strongly focused on the self, but not in the same way as islands. Their needs don't relate to money, power, beauty, youth, or intelligence but rather to emotional regulation. They have a need to depend on someone or something outside for nearly constant contact and reassurance. If the island moves away to self-soothe, the wave moves toward their partner to talk and calm down.

Making a Wave

Wave parents are frequently inconsistent and often unavailable—distracted or preoccupied—or frustrated suddenly with their children's neediness. In addition, they are often poor at self-regulation. Wave parents will expect their children to need and want closeness with them and, alternately, can feel overwhelmed by clinginess and push their children away, thus leaving children to feel wanted and needed sometimes and rejected and punished for being a burden at other times. Wave parents will often reward their children for remaining young, cute, and dependent, discouraging separation and independence. Because of this, wave adults can feel underentitled or underprepared to get what they want. They expect to be disappointed, rejected, punished, and abandoned, which leaves them feeling needy and too much of a burden.

Like their wave parent, they feel at times overwhelmed by their adult responsibilities and angry for having never truly been supported. They feel their autonomy was traded in for a false sense of security by remaining dependent and waiting for their turn.

Additionally, during a critical developmental period known as rapprochement—a time of intense ambivalence for the child—frustration and anger with what is now felt as an imperfect caregiver reaches an apex. The child will typically practice crying for help alternated with rejecting and punishing the caregiver. A wave parent—themselves familiar with rejection, withdrawal, and punishment—may reflexively withdraw from and punish the child in return, therefore reinforcing this type of exchange.

How Waves Interact with Others

Waves fervently seek proximity and love long periods of contact with their partner, unlike islands who tend to avoid proximity and tolerate only abbreviated periods of close contact. Also unlike islands, who don't like to talk a lot about the relationship, waves thrive in this arena. In fact, waves will often calm themselves down by talking to another person. Silence can be a problem for most waves.

Waves tend to be negativistic. Think of negativism as evidence of a strong desire for something and an equally strong fear that those hopes will be dashed. The wave has been jerked around in childhood. It's been a "come here, go away" experience repeatedly, with at least one caregiver. Come-hither cues are sometimes rewarded with warmth and love, but sometimes with frustration, rejection, and abandonment instead. Waves, as children, often experience this caregiver flip-flopping as unreliable and will show signs of anger and resistance when reuniting with the caregiver. Waves, in general, automatically predict loss, and that's when their rejecting, punishing reflexes come to the fore. Negativism, therefore, is a reflex to push away a loved one when predicting disappointment, loss, or abandonment. In a sense, they're *allergic to hope*.[4] As soon as they hope—for reuniting, receiving praise, being reassured—they feel dread, anxiety, and maybe even anger.

Waves are often at their most ambivalent when getting what they want, which stems from an unresolved developmental crisis. Where anchors learn to accept the world as gray, consisting of both good and bad at the same time, waves see things in black and white, which makes it hard for them to make important decisions. They avoid making decisions by remaining ambivalent, but this keeps them in a place of powerlessness. Anger about this lack of control tends to be blamed on the partner. This is like the island's excuse that their secretive, withholding behavior is due to their partner's inability to accept them as they are.

How Waves Restore Internal Peace and Balance

Self-regulation is the ability to manage your emotional and physiological states and regulate your responses to your environment. We're not born with this ability. It's a vital strategy not only for managing the self but also for being in relationship with others. Self-regulation is the only strategy that provides restraint, inhibition, and waiting. If we had no capacity for self-regulation we would be all impulse, aggression, and acceleration. Self-regulation comes online at around ten to twelve months after birth and develops according to various circumstances. Waves tend to have difficulty with self-regulation. As a substitute, waves overrely upon external sources in order to regulate.

External regulation is a normal strategy, present at birth. As infants, we're externally regulated by our caregivers. We don't have an internal mechanism to do otherwise. Therefore, our caregivers externally manage our communications, internal state, sleep cycle, temperature, sense of balance, and much, much more. External regulation continues into adulthood and, again, is normal. Consider going into a classroom and learning from a teacher who is externally regulating you. Or calling a friend when you're upset to help you calm down.

WAVE STATE SHIFTING

From interaction to noninteraction = hard

From noninteraction to interaction = easy

The island runs into relationship problems when relying on autoregulation, whereas the wave runs into relationship problems in the absence of external regulation. While external regulation requires interaction with others, it's still one-sided. It lacks simultaneity. It can overburden a partner who expects reciprocity. Think of the sometimes continuous need for external regulation, a feature that's common to codependent individuals. This strategy of self-care looks and acts relational but is quite similar to that of the island in that the regulation style lacks collaboration and cooperation. It serves the self only.

Waves Value Relationships in the Context of Self
Waves love taking care of others. They love to be around others and are good at seeing more than one point of view. In this way islands and waves have something vital in common. They tend to think in terms of a one-person system that's self-centered, entitled, and outside the bounds of fairness and justice. A wave may express their external regulation by being overly concerned about a friend, staying up all

night talking them off the ledge. But it can also be expressed in the reverse. The distressed wave will call everyone they can in order to be talked down from the ledge. Waves tend to overexpress their emotions and will resort to hyperbole to make their point. Unlike islands, who tend to think in a more linear, logical manner, waves tend to think in a nonlinear and emotion-based manner, and attempt to understand and communicate emotional meaning rather than logic.

Waves and Conflict

Let's examine this in the context of distress. Of the three main states or traits of relating, waves are the most likely to be considered "high maintenance" by their partners. They shift between feeling needy, angry, and guilty that they're too much to handle. Since they rely on external sources to soothe them, they're acutely aware that their neediness can be annoying. Nonetheless, waves can often appear to seek conflict and be unable to let things go. During periods of distress, the wave is less interested in meeting the needs of the relationship and more interested in their own concerns. Unlike islands, who often refuse to look back and remember, waves will be the first to bring up past conflicts, refusing to move forward until past injustices and injuries have been addressed and resolved.

So do you want to marry a wave? Why not? Waves are very relational, often quite warm, affectionate, loving, and exciting. If your wave partner is unaware of their insecure-functioning defensive behaviors and is disinterested in becoming aware, then you should pass on this person. However, if your wave partner is aware and finds their wave defenses as destructive as you do, catch the wave.

I'm a Wave

Me   So tell me something about yourself.

Him   Well, that's a broad question. I don't know where
to begin. I can tell you lots of things. I'm a nice
guy. I care a lot about people. I tend to fall in
love pretty easily. But it seems as if everyone I
meet takes a lot longer.

Me   What do you mean?

Him Before I got engaged, I tended to fall in love easily but often felt that it wasn't returned. I'm a real people person. I like to interact and talk, and I'm really very affectionate. When I'm with someone who isn't affectionate or withholds, it drives me crazy. I tend to be pretty outgoing and some people don't appreciate that. I'm just interested in people. I'm very expressive with my emotions, and when you're on my good side, that's great. But if you get on my bad side, watch out! I say that, but I'm a real pussycat.

Me Tell me about your partner—your fiancée.

Him Well, she's a bit older than I am. Ain't that wild? She's beautiful, of course. But I think she's really a good person, the best person I've ever known. She's smart, successful, not as outgoing as I am, and stable.

Me I understand that you had to wait for her, right? She was married when you met her?

Him Yes, she was. I didn't think we would make it. I felt so insecure. I felt that I was really there for her, but I kept getting this distance, you know. I can't believe I hung in there for almost two years. But the divorce is done, and now we're getting married.

Me So now that stress is over and done with.

Him Well, I guess I got the girl, but she's still in touch with her ex because they have a daughter together. I don't like it and wish he didn't exist. Is that bad? [laughs] Actually, I know that's not right.

Me May I ask you some questions about your childhood?

Him Ask away.

Me When you were a child and you were sick, who took care of you?

Him My mother, of course. She actually was the best when I was sick. She was at her nicest. I think she actually liked it when I was home sick with her. We watched TV shows together and she'd rub my back. To this day I still love that and try to get every partner to do that for me. Anyway, those times are some of my fondest memories. Unfortunately, she wasn't always that way. She was super attentive when I was sick or injured, but at other times she was cranky and irritable. She was like a child so often. I felt like the parent most of the time. I'd be in her room watching TV with her when my father was out of town, because she was lonely. She cried a lot and was depressed. She lost her mother when I was a baby. My father's work takes him away a lot. My mother would complain to me a lot about their personal lives.

Me When you were a child and you got upset, what did your parents do?

Him Well, it depended on if my parents were in good moods. My mother could never tolerate me being upset with her. She'd either cry and make me take care of her, or get angry and punish me by not talking to me for a couple of hours until I made up with her. That would really piss me off. My father would just hand me off to my mother. He was of no help. My dad was an unemotional type. He didn't like being bothered much. If I was upset, like sad upset, my mother would hold me and comfort me, but that was only if she was in a good mood. So often she was preoccupied with her own stuff, her own activities, and with my dad being away . . . well, they would often fight about that at night.

Me When you were a child, who hugged you, held you, rocked you, kissed you?

Him That's easy. My mother. Like I said, she was very affectionate. My father was affectionate too, but selectively. My father was the most affectionate with me after being affectionate with my mother. But never without that. At least not that I can recall.

Me As a child, who put you to bed?

Him My mother. Most of the time at least. She'd come in, tuck me in, and rub my back. I was greedy. I wanted her to continue doing that a long time, because it felt so good. She'd eventually get mad at me and storm out of the room. That was my mother in a nutshell. So childlike. She was there, but then also sometimes resentful of my wanting her. When she was overwhelmed, which was a lot, she had no patience for me. I remember one time she got so mad she pulled over to the side of the road, turned off the car, closed the door, and left me there while she walked down the street. I thought she was gonna leave me for good, but she came back right away.

Me When you were a child, what did your parents' marriage look like to you? Did it look like they were in love?

Him I saw a lot of things. I saw them be affectionate with each other. I saw my mother try very hard to get my father to be affectionate with her. Sometimes he was, sometimes he wasn't. I think my mother was very jealous. I heard them arguing many times about my father and other women around him at work. I don't think he ever did anything, but my mother was always suspicious. I think my father thought of my mother as being too much sometimes. I thought she was too much sometimes.

Me All kids get scared at night when at a certain age. Do you remember getting scared at night?

Him Oh, yes. I would see ghosts in my closet. Actually, I thought I saw them. I would call out for my mother and, generally, she'd come. She'd calm me down and then go back to her room. At other times, when she responded to my calling out, I would go to their room. Sometimes she was warm and comforting, other times she was annoyed and frustrated, and asked my father to put me back in bed.

Me When you were a child and your mother got upset, would it take her a long time to recover?

Him Sometimes it did. Sometimes she'd get really upset or hurt by something I said and she'd just walk away. Even if I was upset she'd get upset back and make it about her. When I got to be a teenager, I just thought she was a baby. I lost respect for her. To this day, she gets upset if I don't call her and then she kind of punishes me by not calling me. She'll say something biting like, "Two can play at that game." At first, when she did that, I couldn't make any sense of what she meant. But that was her getting back at me for something she felt I did. This reminds me, it's something I do with my fiancée a lot. It makes her as angry as my mom made me. I'm very sensitive to being rejected or forgotten about. I'll test her sometimes, just to see if she really loves me. That's not fair, I know, but sometimes I can't stop myself. No matter how close we get, I still feel insecure. I'm still waiting for the other shoe to drop. I think, jeez, I'm just so needy. We often get into fights when we reunite at the end of the day. After I'm away from her all day, I really miss her. I used to call a lot just to feel the connection, but it bugs her. But once we come together, I imagine she will get upset and withdraw. It's like I'm expecting it. When we don't fight, I'll start to fight as a way to reconnect. It's like I don't want things to end.

The Anchor

Anchors are those individuals who already exhibit the traits of secure functioning. Secure individuals tend to come from families that value relationships over everything else. They're fully committed to their relationships, eager to find win-win situations, and generally more able to acclimate and adjust to whatever obstacles they face. Anchors tend to be happy, resilient people who are good at going with the flow.

Making an Anchor

Anchor parents value the integrity of relationships and tend to put relationships first, particularly family relationships. Anchor parents are both secure and autonomous and so they tolerate both dependence and independence without forcing either. Because anchor parents are generally well resourced and emotionally available to their children, their relations are close and intimate but not overbearing, needy, shaming, or guilt inducing. They're good at self-regulating both their emotions and self-esteem and so don't explicitly or implicitly require external regulation from their children. Anchor parents tend to have high expectations with regard to good behavior, cooperation, academic achievement, organization, and goals. However, these parents also provide significant support to match their expectations. In anchor families, performance and physical appearance aren't valued above relationship integrity or harmony. In secure families, parents tend to be good managers of one another; they demonstrate their relationship skills in front of their children and therefore lead by example. These parents will have conflict openly and will also openly repair misunderstandings and hurt feelings promptly. Secure and autonomous families also tend to be affectionate, verbal, expressive, and empathic.

How Anchors Interact with Others

Anchors show and offer more face-to-face, eye-to-eye, and skin-to-skin interaction than waves or islands. They tend to rely upon *interactive regulation*—mutual regulation, or coregulation—wherein partners manage each other's psychobiological state, unconsciously, at rapid speeds. For example, if one partner begins to show signs of distress, the other partner will notice and be responsive. This responsiveness—in both directions—takes place simultaneously and seamlessly as if there were no uncorrected errors or missteps.

In early childhood, caregiver and infant start off using external regulation to manage emotional states. However, once they get going, infant and caregiver will appear to interactively regulate in a give-and-take that's highly engaged and seemingly leaderless. This is the same as the adult version. Interactive regulation is far more continuous and fluid across various positive and negative emotional states between anchor partners than between waves or islands.

How Anchors Restore Inner Peace and Balance

Recall that autoregulation, which is overrelied upon by the island, is a strategy of self-stimulation and self-soothing without the need for another person. External regulation, an overused strategy by the wave, is in one direction at a time and lacks simultaneity. The latter is more akin to what people think of as codependent behavior. Self-regulation, a precondition for the adult version of coregulation, allows individuals to hold impulses, manage frustration, and stay within social engagement under stress. Good self-regulation and apt engagement in mutual regulation are hallmark features of the anchor.

ANCHOR STATE SHIFTING

From interaction to noninteraction = easy

From noninteraction to interaction = easy

Anchors: Centered on Relationship and Attachment Values

Anchors tend to be more attuned to others. They're socially-emotionally intelligent and facile regardless of educational background. They tend to get along with a wide swath of people and personalities. They're more accepting of people and their differences; more curious, focused, and attentive with others. Perhaps their most pronounced features are their eagerness to cooperate and collaborate with others and their appreciation for attachment values. Anchors are naturally inclined to ensure safety and security for their partners, and they're equally inclined to expect the same in return. In this and other ways, they maintain healthy self-entitlements, which includes seeking appropriate, reciprocal relationships with others; advancing their education, careers, and interests; and continually moving toward increasing complexity as human beings. They don't give up easily on people and pursuits they deem good for them. That doesn't mean that anchors are fearful of turning away from people, projects, or things that are harmful or opposed to their values and principles.

Anchors aren't perfect. After all, they're people. They can be quite wave-ish or island-ish. Yet their anchor foundation shows in their relationship values; their continuous fresh psychological insight, honesty, and forthrightness; and their cooperative and collaborative spirit. In contrast to waves and islands, anchors usually feel secure as individuals when they enter into a committed partnership. Because they aren't encumbered by fears of abandonment or engulfment, anchors are more likely to act in a reciprocal, supportive, and relaxed manner with their partner. They tend to be open to understanding how their actions cause distress in the relationship and are prepared to repair hurt feelings or perceived injustices. Anchors draw strength from their relationships and from working as part of a team to handle the myriad challenges life throws at them. Although they enjoy closeness and physical contact, anchors are also secure in themselves and their relationships when they're apart from their partner.

Anchors and Conflict

Anchors do conflict better than islands and waves. While the island tends to withdraw and the wave tends to cling, the anchor is committed to resolve conflict and address distress in a way that's mutually agreeable and satisfying. In this way, they protect their couple bubble. They're dedicated first to moving forward as a team as opposed to getting their own needs met at the expense of the other.

So should you marry an anchor? If you're looking for safety and security, a relationship filled with mutual appreciation and respect, and someone who is there for you when the going gets tough, then yes! Anchors make great partners. But remember, anchors have problems too. All people are annoying, and all relationships are burdensome. Having said that, anchors are less burdened by memories and fears that come with dependency-type relationships. We're attracted to and attract those with whom we recognize and with whom we're familiar. If you're in the insecure camp, you may find yourself recognizing vulnerabilities of insecurity. Whether you're on the clingy or distancing side of insecure adaptation, the bottom-line fear is abandonment. Anchors have abandonment fears and engulfment fears, but they're not as pushed around by those fears as waves or islands.

Now here's the really good part. Secure-functioning principles are what matter in adult attachment relationships. Secure functioning assumes symmetry of stakes, power, and influence. It assumes that the two parties are adults who understand that, in order to survive and thrive, there must be order; there must be cooperation and collaboration; and there must always be mutual respect, high regard, and loyalty. As secure-functioning partners, your fates are linked, your futures are interconnected. You don't have to be perfect at this. You simply have to be good enough. In this case, good enough *is* perfect. The truth is, in a secure-functioning relationship, chances are very high that you will pull each other toward the anchor culture within a relatively short period of time.

I'm an Anchor

> **Me** So tell me about yourself.
>
> **Him** Let's see. I'm fifty-eight years old, I'm married with two grown children. I'm a political science professor [at a well-known New England university]. I also consult as part of a government think tank in Washington, DC—and yes, I love what I do.
>
> **Me** I'm going to ask some questions about your childhood. Would that be okay?

Him	Sure, go right ahead.
Me	When you were a child, before the age of twelve, who hugged you, held you, rocked you, kissed you?
Him	When I was little, I remember my parents being very affectionate with me. They still are. My best memories are of my mother holding me in her lap and scratching my back. I just loved that. I often ask my wife to do that today. [laughs] She'll look at me with a gleam in her eye and then give me a kiss. My father put his arm around me a lot. I remember that. I also remember him putting me up on his shoulders. Come to think of it, my dad would also put me on his lap, and we'd watch TV together.
Me	What shows did you watch?
Him	Westerns. We'd watch *Bonanza*, *The Rifleman* —shows like that. I remember popcorn and those shows and my dad.
Me	When you were a child, which parent played with you—just you?
Him	My father played catch with me in the backyard. I loved doing that with him. My mom taught me how to play gin rummy. I also played with my grandfather . . . gin rummy. I spent special time alone with my father, going fishing and camping. I also had special time with my mother as well. We'd go to the movies or take a drive to the beach.
Me	Were you around your parents a lot as a child?
Him	Both my parents had to work for a living. We weren't wealthy; we were a mid- to lower-class family. We had each other. My older brother and I always looked forward to the evening when we would sit around the dinner table and talk about our day. Sometimes my parents would discuss the future and how they were going to accomplish things. Sometimes my

father would say, "This isn't just about your mother and me. We all have to pull together." I remember feeling and thinking that my parents loved each other. Almost every night and every weekend we would drive somewhere, such as the beach. I always thought they were doing that for my brother and me, but later I found out they loved doing these things together as a couple and a family.

Me When you were a child, what did your parents' marriage look like to you? Did it look like they were in love?

Him To me? Yes. They were affectionate with each other and very respectful. I learned a lot about how to work as a team by watching my parents. I remember them fighting, even yelling and screaming at each other, but they would always make up right away, and each would admit what they did to cause the fight.

Me How did your parents react when you got angry?

Him The same thing would happen between me and my mother. I remember getting angry with her when I was a little kid. Sometimes she'd get angry back, but most of the time she'd just hear me out. Then she'd say something that made me feel better, even if it wasn't what I wanted to hear. When it came to my being angry as a kid, my father would just listen to me while he worked in the garage. My brother and I would get into fights and my parents would make us work it out. At the time I hated that, but now I think it was the greatest thing they could've done.

Me Was performance and expectation a big focus when you were little?

Him My parents expected me and my brother to work hard and shoot for the stars. They also supported us by sitting down and helping us work out solutions. When we would fail, like in school or Little League, there was no judgment. I was expected to do it, but I knew my parents valued our relationships more than whether I performed well. "I want you to feel good about yourself, to feel accomplished. Not for me; for you," my father would say. Both he and my mother were hard workers. But they never complained. They saw people as mostly good with some random bad apples.

Me When you were a child, did it feel as if your mother and father would really see you—see who you were?

Him I always had a sense that my mom and dad could really see me. My mother could always tell if I was trying to get away with something or telling a fib. She'd just smile at me and look me in the eyes, and I knew I was caught red-handed. As a teenager I hated that feature, but I came to appreciate her ability to read me. Sometimes I thought my father wasn't paying attention. At times he was preoccupied with his work and hobbies. I used to complain about my father's aloofness, but I later came to understand that was his way. I knew he loved me. And I knew he knew as much about me as my mother. I would hear them talking to each other about us—kind of giving each other an update.

I saw my parents laugh, struggle, get angry, cry, but I never felt that I had to worry about them. They seemed really good with each other, and I learned a lot from them—how to work through differences and how to be loving. I think that's why my marriage to Missy is so good. It's easy. Like my parents, we fight, we cry, we push and pull on each other, we laugh, but the solidarity of our relationship is never in question. Now we have two children of our own and often do the things my parents did with me. I remember the stories my father would tell me at bedtime, the songs my mother would sing around the house, and the games we would all play together. Was it all perfect? No, not nearly. But they helped me deal with this world and taught me how to love.

SO . . . ARE YOU AN ISLAND, AN ANCHOR, OR A WAVE?

If both you *and* your partner believe you to be mostly cooperative, collaborative, and good humored; if you mostly abide by principles of fairness, justice, and sensitivity; and if you see relationships as your highest value, you're probably an anchor. Remember, anchors can be wave-ish or island-ish, but they're also all of what I just described. To learn more, you can take the Adult Attachment Interview (AAI) with a trained interviewer and have your interview coded and interpreted by a reliable AAI coder.[5]

Unless you're an attachment nerd, this last step is unnecessary. The purpose of this chapter is to help you in your relationship and provide you with some ideas about managing yourself and your partner. This material should never be used to diagnose yourself or your partner, as one would with a mental disorder. Nor should it be used to demean, dismiss, or attack yourself or your partner. Nor should it be used to pride yourself by calling yourself an anchor. No human being is anything if not complex and difficult to fully grasp. Anchors, islands, and waves are ideas, not real people. Use these ideas for understanding yourself and your partner and not for judgment, criticism, or pigeonholing. This whole attachment business is just a piece in the relationship puzzle. There's much, much more to human relationships than attachment.

THE MATTER OF UNRESOLVED
TRAUMA OR LOSS

Unresolved trauma or loss affects how someone feels and behaves, but neither fits into the nautical motif of island, anchor, and wave. Unresolved trauma or loss brings other challenges into the system—challenges that are much more complex than simply whether a partner is secure or insecure. Generally speaking, unresolved trauma or loss leads to what attachment researchers call *disorganization* or *disorientation*. You can be an anchor, island, or wave with disorganization.

Everyone has experienced loss and some kind of trauma in their life. However, some of these losses or traumas occur very early in childhood when the brain is developing. The problem isn't really the loss or the traumatic event but rather that the individual who experiences such an event doesn't have an adult—someone considered safe or sensitive—to turn to, someone who can respond in a timely manner to help regulate the experience. The child (with a child's brain) is left to their own devices to adapt to the intensity of the experience. That's what causes the unresolved part, and these unresolved injuries influence further development, especially in the areas of safety and security.

Waves and islands suffer from a different kind of interpersonal or relational trauma. For instance, the wave experienced inconsistency, rejection, withdrawal, and punishment. But at other times, the wave experienced lots of love and affection. It makes sense that the adult wave might feel extraordinarily sensitive to any signs of withdrawal or rejection and that abandonment is one of their greatest fears. The island may have experienced a lot of neglect or consistent pressure to perform or to appear a certain way. Islands have often been the recipients of criticism and attack. It's no wonder they're highly sensitive to feeling attacked and criticized.

Nonetheless, both islands and waves have predictable backgrounds with predictable parenting, and their behavior going forward is also predictable. Not so with some individuals who experience disorganized states due to unresolved trauma or loss in early childhood. Whereas insecure individuals are thought to be the recipients of insensitive parenting, disorganized individuals may have been the recipients of frightening parenting or frightening experiences when they were young.[6]

I want to caution the reader to beware of overidentifying with what I'm describing. It's very easy for us to begin imagining this or that about our childhoods. Remember what I've said about the brain: it makes up shit, especially in the absence of memory and real experience. Don't go looking for things that didn't actually happen. All of us have pockets of unresolved issues just waiting to pop up when triggered unexpectedly. We all have had experiences we didn't think through or grieve. That's not what I'm talking about here.

We're hurt by people and we're healed by people. It's important that individuals who have experienced early trauma or loss seek help with someone knowledgeable in these areas. A partner may not be suitable for this purpose. Yet there are many cases of partners, both with unresolved trauma or loss, who fight with each other and want to be in a secure-functioning relationship. Processing the amount of unresolved material that I'm talking about here doesn't necessarily mean that a secure-functioning relationship is out of reach—quite the opposite. However, for the relationship to succeed you will want to understand the complications from your partner's or your past.

What Are Those Complications?

Folks who have a lot of unresolved trauma are more likely than others to respond to threat cues in the environment. These cues are picked up from dangerous facial expressions, movements, gestures, and vocal tone, as well as dangerous words and phrases. This may make relationships more difficult for them because of their hypervigilance and hypersensitivity to threat cues. If both partners have unresolved issues, this hypersensitivity can multiply and interfere with the couple's sense of safety and security.

Frankie, a male in his thirties, was engaged to Margaret, a female in her late twenties. As a child—from about ages five to nine—Frankie had been molested repeatedly by an uncle. There was no one for him to go to, so he never told anyone about it. Margaret complained that Frankie would often become physically rigid when she reached out to touch him. He'd pull away quickly and change the subject and the focus of attention. She also complained that they had trouble in bed. Frankie complained that Margaret was disrespectful of his "space" and described her as hypersexual. Because Frankie felt a tremendous amount of shame, he was unable to talk to Margaret. Not only that, he didn't really understand his behavior because he'd avoided this unresolved experience. His almost constant fear and anxiety about getting close, especially physically, to Margaret, compounded by his fear that she'd break off the engagement, got him to come in for couple therapy. Working through this early trauma with Margaret helped both of them. But more unresolved experiences remained, such as Frankie never feeling protected by either parent and his continual fear of being "prey."

Cheryl and Jody, both in their midforties, were about to be married. Cheryl complained that Jody would never pay attention and could never remember important things. This became somewhat of a deal breaker because Cheryl believed that Jody either had a memory problem or she simply didn't care enough about the relationship to pay attention. When they came in for couple counseling, we did some exercises to test short-term memory. What we all discovered was that Jody's memory was just fine. She also cared deeply for Cheryl. But she felt under constant attack by Cheryl, who continually complained about her forgetfulness. Interestingly, Cheryl didn't do so well in the memory test, but the reason wasn't her memory. She had so much unresolved trauma from early childhood around abandonment that whenever she perceived that Jody was withdrawing in any measure, Cheryl would incorrectly appraise Jody's thoughts, feelings, and intentions. She also misremembered events.

We're all creatures of adaptation. That's what we do. As children, we don't get to choose the family we're born into. We simply must adapt in order to survive. That's nature. There's no good or bad, right or wrong, healthy or unhealthy in nature. Our impressions are subjective and based on past experiences and perceptions. Individuals with uncommonly strong unresolved histories have also adapted to their environment. However, the earlier the adaptation, the more the brain and the body are affected at the cellular and genetic level. Without the ability to process that experience with the help of others, more changes will occur in the brain and body. Therefore personality, perception, and important brain functions, such as memory, reality testing, and error correction, become impaired and altered.

The signs and symptoms of substantive unresolved trauma or loss are often the following (this isn't a conclusive list):

- chronic dissociation

- paranoia

- hypervigilance

- episodes of substantial confusion or disorientation

- rapid shifts toward hyperarousal or hypoarousal, or both

- episodes of collapse, stilling, fainting, losing time

- poor recovery from distress states

- derealization

- depersonalization

Once again, please do be careful when reading this that you don't diagnose yourself or your partner from the material that I've given you. If you or your partner believes that what I'm describing here may be present in either or both of you, seek a professional who can help you determine if there's a real problem. Otherwise keep it in the back of your mind to help you better understand how past traumas affect others.

Don't use these ideas as a bat with which to hit your partner over the head. The purpose of this section isn't to label anybody. Islands, waves, anchors, and folks with disorganization are all descriptions of generalized patterns of behavior. I've described them to help you get along with others, not the opposite. Everything said here is generalized, and the research behind it is far more complex and nuanced. It exists only to study people as a way to help understand aggregates of people. My whole point in this book is to help you with your partner distinguish pathological tendencies from those that are actually normal and natural human tendencies.

WHAT WAS YOUR EARLIEST RELATIONSHIP LIKE?

Primary romantic attachments are worlds apart from other relationships, except the earliest ones with our caregivers. Consider the caregivers you had or remember before the age of twelve. Why? Because after twelve we shift into adolescence. At around ten to twelve years of age we get a brain "upgrade" whereby the world looks different to us. We start to care about peer groups more, to become more aware of the culture around us, such as clothes and music. From about ages thirteen to fifteen we enter into adolescence proper, when we receive more brain upgrades and go through another round of challenges similar to those we went through at ages three and four and then again at around ages seven and eight. The reason for adolescent turmoil isn't what we usually blame: hormones. To be sure, hormones affect teen bodies; however, teens' uneven brain development is at the root of most adolescent behavioral and emotional tumult.

Attachment is a good model for helping us understand how we're likely to feel and behave in a primary attachment relationship. It's important to remember that attachment theory, like all theoretical models, is flawed and wasn't (originally) designed for adult couples. Nonetheless, since it was designed for the "original" couple (infant and caregiver), it's still applicable. Keep in mind that attachment changes throughout the lifespan. It's malleable, and though partners can pull each other into secure attachment, the opposite can also be true.

Remember that attachment only has to do with safety and security in our most primary relationships. The expectations in these relationships, like it or not, resemble the earliest ones and our memories around dependency—both good and bad. When using the term *insecure*, we mean there remains some fears or apprehensions about dependency and all it embodies. It informs how we will seek proximity with our partner; tolerate sustained periods of physical and emotional contact; manage conflict and disagreement; and view reciprocity, mutuality, and fairness. Insecure attachment will also affect how we experience love and eroticism and behave in these matters. (We cover sex in an upcoming chapter.)

How do you and your partner know if you're an island, an anchor, or a wave? By *how strongly and consistently you act* on fears of abandonment, rejection, dismissiveness, intrusion, threats to your autonomy, and so on. But remember, folks, where there's one, there's the other. No one operates alone. If you're an island and you meet a more severe island, you're going to act like a wave. If you're a wave and you meet a stronger wave than yourself, you're going to act like an island. If you're secure and island-ish or wave-ish and your partner is an island, your inner wave is going to come out strongly.

6

HOW WELL DO YOU
KNOW EACH OTHER?

The two of you are in each other's care; therefore it's incumbent upon both of you to know each other as well as you know yourselves, perhaps better. Does your partner know you better than anyone else in your life? What about in the reverse?

Some years ago I wrote about what I call the *pseudo-secure couple*. These couples appear terrific, even secure functioning, but on the outside only. On the inside, they are strangers to each other. Several of these couples, many of them together for decades, would come in to counseling due to a reveal of an earth-shaking, never-before-known secret. It could be about multiple, years-long affairs, the existence of another marriage and family, a secret offshore account, or something else of great magnitude.

What amazed me was that the partners seemed to know nothing about each other. I knew more in one hour than they appeared to know over the course of thirty years. How could that be? Most frequently it was due to their mutual disinterest in knowing the truth. These partners found comfort in knowing each other on a surface level, both satisfied with the positive nature of their affiliation, as if they never progressed past the initial idealization of the courtship phase. Their avoidance and ability to remain content with an idea of themselves and the relationship concealed their reality until the discovery of a life-altering secret.

There are plenty of examples involving romantic affairs whereby a partner claims a "stranger" knows more about them than their spouse. How does that happen? Is it the spouse's fault for not being curious? Is it the partner's fault for not opening up and revealing their true self? Some people, especially avoidant individuals (islands), prefer to spread around information about themselves, never allowing one person to know everything. Others wait for people to draw information out of them rather than offering it freely.

If you're in each other's care, are you competent? Are you an expert on your partner? If not, why? Is it because you think it unnecessary? Or perhaps you want to be known, but you're not too interested in knowing. Consider how you learn about yourself. You don't do that by yourself on your own but rather through other people. Get to know your partner really well. Study them. Pay attention. Just because you *think* you know them, you may not, so keep watching, listening, sherlocking.

ARE YOU RIGHT FOR EACH OTHER?

You've decided to marry, but are you right for each other? Many people make lists to describe their ideal partner beyond physicality: the way they think, feel, and view the world. But these lists don't always consider the qualities that will support a happy, thriving long-term partnership. If you've made a list, be honest. Did it include any physical features? What about professional or financial success? What about similar interests? Maybe you were also looking for someone who wanted (or didn't want) children. Or maybe they had to be of a certain religion or ethnic group. Even if you're not a list maker, you must have thought about who that ideal person would be: blonde or brunette, tall or short, thin or heavy, outgoing or reserved, funny or serious, wild or down-to-earth.

While physical looks, wealth and ambition, religion, and personality may be important to you, none of these features guarantee a truly happy long-term relationship. With time, all these things can change, and if the relationship is insecure-functioning, can partners ever really be happy? Let's talk about the common reasons people marry and whether these stand the test of time, starting with an example of a bad match.

Bonnie and Derek, both twenty-four, are getting married for the first time. They came in for premarital counseling. Neither made lists, but when asked, Bonnie described what she wanted in a mate.

Bonnie   I want someone who will be considerate and talk to me nicely, with respect. He must dress well, have manners, be successful, and treat my parents with respect.

Me   What does that mean, be successful?

Bonnie   It means he's someone who I can respect; who's doing something admirable. [pause] But also makes a lot of money [giggles]. That's important too.

Me   How important?

Bonnie   Uh . . . [She looks at Derek] very important.

Derek   She has expensive tastes. [They both laugh.]

Me   [to Bonnie] Anything else?

Bonnie   [looking at Derek] Um . . . he must be sexy and handsome. [She coyly bites one side of her lip.]

Derek   Which I am [he says with his chest comically puffed out; both laugh].

Me   What about you, Derek?

Derek   Well . . . she must be beautiful. Sexy. Not too smart [laughs]. No, just kidding. She has to be independent because I don't like clingy women. She has to be loyal and stay close to me.

Me   What does that mean?

Derek   It means I don't want her going out with friends, just me. I want her at home with me and not around other men. She's too sexy.

Bonnie   [with a feigned look of indignation] What? I'm not the one who cheats! [to me] He cheated on me before and after we got engaged. He's slept with everyone and can tell you about it.

Me   [to Derek] Is that true?

> **Derek**   Absolutely. But I was immature. And she was busy
> building her business. I was around lots of pretty
> girls, what can I say? I'm a bad boy. But she
> kissed somebody and won't tell me who. Ask her
> about that.
>
> **Bonnie**   What a pathetic dick you are, Derek. You're a
> misogynous pig. I can't believe I'm marrying you.
> [She folds her arms and turns away with a smile;
> he's smiling too.]

I think you get the gist here. Are any alarms going off in your head? We have a big problem for several reasons, only one of which has to do with cheating. Both partners' reasons for being together are focused on ideas that are unsustainable as opposed to having a vision for the *relationship*. It's all about self needs. Nothing about character, moral judgment, or principles that serve any kind of mutual good. And neither seem aware of how their own behavior impacts the relationship or the other's well-being.

Bonnie wants someone who is respectful, yet she talks to him disrespectfully, as if the notion of consideration and respect goes out the window if it concerns *her* behavior. Derek wants her to remain faithful yet is unrepentant about his own faithlessness. He picked her for her independence yet insists that she remain at home with or without him. What really worries me is their cavalier attitudes about their stances. Issues that *really should* concern them—trust, independence, mutuality—seem to be laughing matters. Yet I know they're deeply serious about their fundamental disagreement about such things.

In case you're attributing their attitudes as normal for their age, consider the following example. Mara and Pete are also twenty-four years old and getting married for the first time. They've come in for premarital counseling.

> **Mara**   I wanted someone with a good moral compass,
> someone I could trust to do the right thing in
> most situations. I think Pete and I share common
> values about people and the world, which is

amazing to me. I have very high standards in this area. I want someone who values relationship and wants to make our marriage the most important thing. I saw that with my parents and always wanted that for myself and my partner. I tend to think about how we will be together in the world, with our families and our children.

Pete Yeah, I agree. Mara and I aren't religious. Neither of us came from strong religious backgrounds, but both of us value service; we like to help people, even though we do it differently. We've talked a lot about this. Both of us want to build a life together, as a team. We work well together. We're both good to our friends and families. People like us and want to be around us. We're proud of that.

Mara We're already best friends. We help each other with our careers and other problem areas. We're equals and find that incredibly hot. We really take good care of each other.

Pete Yeah, we protect each other. You have to do that if you want to make it as a couple.

I couldn't have said it better. Do you get alarms going off in your head this time? You shouldn't. Both are talking about personal and mutual principles, a shared vision of the relationship and its future. Though they're only twenty-four, they sound more mature than many older couples. True, they come from families with good examples of coupling, but they already come to the table with a secure-functioning relationship, so we can predict good things for them.

Without a sense of safety and security, you might ask yourself, what's the point? What holds you guys together? What do you do for each other that you couldn't pay somebody to do? If you think of your survival unit as a structure that protects you from the weather, how strong is your unit? What kinds of winds can you survive? Are you ready for all types of conditions?

WHY DO YOU WANT TO MARRY?

The reasons people decide to marry can be quite diverse. Some responses are incompatible with long-term success. Taking them one at a time, I will discuss each of the common reasons people marry in the context of secure functioning, including:

- "I love him/her."

- "We have so much in common."

- "We're so passionate."

- "I've always wanted children."

- "I'm getting old, so if not now, when?"

- "I want a relationship where we help each other to survive and thrive."

I Love Him/Her

Expressing your love for your partner is nice, but what do you actually mean when you say, "I love you?" What does love mean to you? If your partner was from Mars, how would you explain this? Break it down and be very specific. For you and your partner, is love the juicy, exciting, over-the-moon experience? Is it infatuation? Is it an idea of love or is it specific to your person? Is the love you feel coming from mutual respect, real admiration, and absolute trust in your partner and who your partner really is? In other words, is the love you feel earned through your partner's deeds? *Love*, like so many words, is meaningless without specifics, details, examples, and a fully thought-out explanation.

EXERCISE
What Is Love?

Talk rigorously about what love means to you. Do this face to face
and eye to eye. Watch each other like hawks as you each respond to
the following prompts:

- Pretend your partner is an alien from another planet. Make
  them understand what love is and what it isn't.

- Explain to your partner why you love them and be specific.
  Don't hedge, take shortcuts, generalize, or say what you
  think your partner wants to hear.

We Have So Much in Common

Partners are usually more alike than not, and we often marry someone
with attributes shared by our self, parents, friends, and previous partners.
Yes, opposites attract, but not on all levels. I'm in complete agreement
with couple therapist Harville Hendrix that we pick our partners based
on recognition and familiarity.[1] Too much familiarity breeds boredom,
but too much unfamiliarity breeds homesickness. In my experience,
these two problems tend to occur with younger partners who are more
invested in values and traditions from their families of origin. As we age,
we tend to be more flexible, worldly, experienced, and less beholden to
rigid ideas and traditions. Of course, that's not always the case.

   If you believe that what you two have in common is what binds
you, think again. As you travel through time together it's common
for interests to shift, fade, or change with time. If you're together
only because you share common interests, you may not last very long.
Drifting away from common interests can lead to major differences in
values and worldview. Likewise, common interests can be the cause of
the drift. A partner may become deeply religious, change their political leanings, or want to have an open marriage. Couples must have a
reason to be together beyond common interests, eroticism, love, kids,
or just plain convenience. Couples who stay together for the long term
have something much bigger that unites and binds them.

What Do You Have in Common?

Take turns explaining to each other what you think you have in common. Besides interests, hobbies, careers, religion, or goals, explain your vision for:

- How people should act and react to each other

- The right and wrong behaviors and attitudes in a relationship

- How this relationship should be governed—should you be equals with equal power, equal status, and equal authority over each other?

We're So Passionate

The first part of most relationships is marked with excitement, novelty, and passion. As your relationship becomes more routine, the novelty starts to wane. There's no way to recapture that exact feeling of novelty, and passion will change. Lust and passion, or sex alone, aren't ingredients that can sustain a long-term thriving marriage. While there are ways to cultivate passion and novelty in your partnership, it's the connection, not the passion, that's most important.

I've Always Wanted Children

I've met many individuals and couples whose main reason for entering a committed partnership is to have children. That's fine. But if this is your primary reason for pair-bonding, make sure your partner is in it for the exact same reason—and that you've discussed your desires around family in depth. Why? Because if your partner has always dreamed of finding their true love and children are a secondary dream, they may be very disappointed to find out that your dreams are different. Other times, differences in desires for family are much harder to resolve, which is why it's so important when you're considering long-term partnership to dig deep into this topic before marriage.

Children—to Have or Have Not?

Have a serious, in-depth conversation about bringing children into your relationship. Are the two of you a secure-functioning couple inviting a child to join your party? Are you bringing a child into your relationship to serve some other purpose?

Have an honest conversation or debate as to what is and will be your highest priority. Is it (or will it be) the child or children? Will it be your partner relationship? Are you both absolutely on the same page regarding your highest priority? Are you dodging, avoiding, complying, short-changing, or cutting corners on this issue?

I'm Getting Older, So If Not Now, When?

While it's understandable to feel the pressure of time, urgency is never a good reason to commit to anyone or anything. Pick wrongly and you will soon have another problem. (Read this book and think well before you leap.) I've witnessed many a male and female defend their partner choice with pressures that have nothing to do with secure functioning: "My biological clock is ticking like a time bomb, and I'm not likely to find anyone better in the near future so . . ." Or "Everyone says I'm getting too old to be single and playing around; it's time I grow up. Plus, all my friends are married with children." Or "I'm not going to find my 'Prince Charming' anyway, so I might as well go with him."

Each of these statements conveys a fatalistic attitude that's bound to cause issues in a relationship. First, nobody wants to feel synonymous with leftovers. Second, you will forever feel cheated out of the relationship (or rather, person) of your so-called dreams. Third, it's simply not secure functioning to go with a committed relationship just because time's a-wasting and so "why not?" Not accepting each other as is—that's one of the deal breakers in any relationship. How can you accept your soon-to-be spouse as is knowing you settled for second (or third or fourth) best?

Does that mean you should only say yes to marrying your dream person? As we've already established, that's a bad idea. Let's go back to our original question: Are you right for each other? Remember what that really means. The two of you are pointing in the same direction, you share the same vision on big-ticket items, and you have created shared principles that you both believe in.

I Want a Relationship Where We Help Each Other to Survive and Thrive

Here's my take on the reason to get married: Think survival unit. To thrive together you must first survive together. You both get to be more than you would otherwise be on your own because you're potentially more powerful and effective in the world together than you would be alone. Your differences offer checks and balances, something that wouldn't happen if you were alone. The two of you, as a secure-functioning team, can be a force to be reckoned with. You can handle anyone and most anything. If you consider yourselves a survival unit, it will help you get things in perspective and give you a sense of priority.

As you read through the reasons why couples marry, I hope you can see that the most important reason to marry is because you want to become a thriving survival unit. Marriage for the sake of marriage is akin to planting a garden in quicksand. Other aspects such as passion, common interests, and the desire to have children become less important over time.

TELLS

Sherlocking depends on your ability to find your partner's "tells"—body and facial movements (or lack thereof) that give someone away. In poker games, expert players look for tells in their opponents to help them discover bluffing. A bluffing person might scratch their nose, shift their eyes, or adjust their position in their chair. Everyone has tells. Our bodies respond even when we don't want to reveal ourselves. A careful observer can detect tells, especially with their partner.

Tells are very personal and idiosyncratic. What does that lower lid twitch signal when they say or hear certain words or ideas? What just made their upper face still? What triggered that throat-clearing sound? Why did they just stop moving their hand in midsentence? Why did they just slow their speech? Now be careful with this. Just because you notice something doesn't mean that you know the target or source of that person's thoughts or feelings. In other words, all you can trust is that you saw or heard something, so don't start jumping to conclusions. Having said that, knowing your partner's tells takes time, as does noticing when a change takes place and under what circumstances. If your partner always makes a sniffing sound every time they talk about their ex-spouse or partner, that probably is a tell. But of what does it tell? You don't know yet. You could ask your partner how they feel whenever talking about this person. This will eventually help you understand these shifts and changes.

EXERCISE
The Lying Game

Sit across from each other, close enough so you can read each other's face and body. As we've been doing, start with complete silence, maintaining eye contact for a few moments. Settle. Then one of you tells a true story and then a false story. The true story must be completely true. The false story must be completely false.* After you've said both versions, have your partner guess which one is true or false. Switch turns. Repeat until you and your partner can detect physical behaviors (tells) that might tip you off to truth or lie telling. Here are some ideas for stories:

- What's your favorite memory from childhood? Why is it your favorite?

- What sport do you love the most and why?

---

*It's sometimes very difficult to tell a complete lie without adding something that's true. Just do your best. The really good liars always tell lots of truth with their lies. It helps them keep from showing tells.

- What music do you love the most and why? Who are your favorite and least favorite artists?

- What's your favorite movie and why? Who's your favorite and least favorite actor?

- What's something your partner doesn't know about you?

THE NEWLYWED GAME

A game show called *The Newlywed Game* began airing in the midsixties. Three couples competed by answering questions such as "What side of the bed does your spouse sleep on?" or "What bothers you most about your mother-in-law?" The couple was expected to supply the same answers, and the couple with the most number of correct answers won a new washer-dryer or a honeymoon cruise, and so forth. While the show's questions were obviously set up to cause some friction among the newlyweds, the casual observer could easily tell which couple knew each other thoroughly, how the couple interacted when distressed, and whether the couple seemed to be in it together or if one was at risk for being thrown under the bus.

In a secure-functioning relationship, maintaining your couple bubble is paramount. Many of the couples on *The Newlywed Game* sacrificed their bubble to get in the last word or have a laugh at their partner's expense. While they often knew each other's preferences and simple pleasures, they also often ignored the other's fears, boundaries, and vulnerabilities. There were threats to the safety and security of the individual contestants, and many lacked the ability to repair any potential damage to their relationship. In order to operate happily within this dyadic milieu, you need to carry, with great care, the owner's manual for your partner. You know things about the other no one else knows. You know what to do to calm or excite them, how to predict your partner, and how to handle them.

How do you write this owner's manual? One step in building that guidebook is to figure out how well you know each other. I would like you to examine your background and childhood experiences for areas that could get in the way of this. Because the primitives run the show, filling in blanks often without your realizing it, it's important to distinguish whether your partner has done something today to upset you or make you angry, or if the root cause stems from your childhood—for example, a time when you were neglected or suffered another threat or trauma.

Let's start by taking an inventory of the things that push your buttons. Andrea loves to eat at nice restaurants, and Terry loves to take her. Andrea is always on time, feeling it's an imposition and even a sign of disrespect when others are late. Terry has never been a slave to the clock and likes to take life spontaneously. He's often late, and he often forgets commitments. As Andrea waits in the five-star restaurant to celebrate their anniversary, she starts to panic when he's fifteen minutes late. Andrea's a wave, and often fears her partner will abandon her. She needs face time with Terry to feel love and connection, and she tends to feel uncomfortable when separated from him. Conversely, Terry's an island. He fears a clingy partner and feels trapped when expected to be somewhere on time. Not realizing this about each other, Terry and Andrea fight just about every time they meet in a restaurant for a meal.

What fears and limitations from childhood affect your partner today? Here are some questions to ask yourself, which will lead to insights you can share with each other:

- Do you fear being trapped? Do you fear being abandoned?

- Do you need time to yourself? Do you feel uncomfortable when your partner leaves you alone for long periods of time?

- Do you fear intimacy? Do you crave it?

- As a child, were you punished when you spoke your mind? Were you encouraged?

- Do you or your partner have feelings of low self-esteem or self-worth?

If Andrea and Terry had a more complete owner's manual for each other, they could avoid a lot of conflict, especially at mealtime. These kinds of issues are deeply rooted and easily activated. You could say they're kryptonite to your partner. Before you wonder how many hot buttons your partner has, let me assure you that most of the patients I've seen in my practice have only three or four issues that are juicy enough to derail them. These are typically fears, vulnerabilities, or insecurities that have plagued them for most of their lives.

BIDS FOR ATTENTION

We seek proximity with our parents, partners, or children by making eye contact, beckoning, calling out, and wanting to talk. These are called *bids for attention*.[2] Contact maintenance refers to how long the child or adult can maintain physical, eye, or other close contact with a primary other. Anchors, having nothing to fear with closeness or distance, tend to seek proximity and maintain contact without any distress. Waves tend to do a lot of proximity seeking and can maintain physical contact for long periods. Islands can be expected to be more proximity avoiding and to loathe maintaining physical contact for lengthy periods (sex excluded).

Gazing into each other's eyes for five minutes (or more) without speaking stresses the contact maintenance axis. If either of you have difficulty in this area, this exercise will alert you to that problem. Be careful, though; things aren't often as they seem. One of you may want to avert your gaze or do something to break contact because of the other's anxiety. When two people are this physically close with eye contact involved, partners will experience something called *resonance*, a normal human phenomenon of nonverbal communication, and something called *affect* or *somatic contagion*, which means partners can "catch" each other's body sensations and emotions, such as anxiety. If one partner is highly anxious, the other experiences their own along with their partner's anxiety, both amplifying the other. The partner who doesn't have a problem with eye contact will avert their eyes, unaware they're turning away, to reduce their partner's stress. Crazy, huh?

In order to build your owner's manual, you must learn your partner's cues moment to moment. One way to do this is to sit directly across from your partner, close enough to see each other's pupils expand and contract. Simply gaze into each other's eyes. Getting comfortable with eye contact is key in establishing secure attachment with each other. The brain loves a face in close-up. Our close-up vision drinks in the fine muscle movements of a face and the dancing of the eyes. As is often attributed to Shakespeare, the eyes are the windows to the soul. Modern neuroscientists might say the eyes are the windows to the autonomic nervous system. When you look into your partner's eyes you're also looking deeply into their nervous system. A face in close-up is never boring; it reveals endless detail about a person's mental and emotional states. There's always something to discover about your partner when you eye gaze.

EYE CONTACT

In the attachment world, making and maintaining eye contact is a fundamental way we communicate love, interest, and emotion. We tend to fall in love through the eyes—with our babies, children, and partners (even pets). Eye contact is a powerful connector. It's also one of the ways in which we can read others. Eye contact is highly stimulating and can be very difficult for some people. Sustained eye contact, even with one's partner, can lead to increased anxiety, panic, sadness, tearfulness, depression, shame, and anger.

Here are some reasons you may encounter problems with sustained eye gazing:

No one made loving eye contact with you as a child. Mothers who frequently held their babies away from their bodies or turned them to face outward set the stage for decreased eye contact in adulthood. If eye contact is difficult for you, it may be that you didn't receive a great deal of eye contact as an infant and child.

A parent or other authority figure used eye contact to intimidate you. It's a sad fact that eye contact, which should be used for love, can also be used for abuse. Yet some of us had early experiences where eye contact was used as a method of intimidation or aggression. Doing so repeatedly, especially in the eyes of a loving partner, can rewire the experience into something relaxing and comforting.

A parent or other authority figure used prolonged eye contact to monitor or shame you. Some of us were looked at with less than loving eyes too much of the time. Eye contact then becomes overly exposing because the other is looking inside you, without your permission, and not in a good way. It feels as if they're criticizing you, observing your defective parts.

A parent or other early caregiver "chased your eyes" or was insensitive to your cues. Some caregivers demand eye contact by "chasing your eyes." They're insensitive to their child's cues of discomfort or overstimulation. On the receiving end of this, the child feels trapped. Once grown, eye contact continues to feel like entrapment, which can feel threatening.

A parent or other early caregiver behaved as if they could see you, but they couldn't. There are caregivers who project their thoughts, feelings, and intentions on their child, which results in repeated misattunement. The result is being seen inaccurately while feeling invaded and intruded upon.

Regardless of why you might be gaze averse, you can train yourself to acclimate to sustaining eye contact with your partner, with the eye contact–avoidant partner in charge of how long you maintain your gaze. But don't avoid this, at least not with your partner. Be curious about what pushes you around inside, and if it's appropriate, push back.

READING YOUR PARTNER'S FACE

We could do a whole chapter on reading faces, but that will be for another book. For now, I want you to start paying attention to your partner's face. Really look closely. As you sit across from them, notice any changes as you and your partner talk. This could be while you're at dinner, when sitting in your living space, or just as an exercise to learn each other's facial "tells." You're looking for small changes that may give away your partner's internal experiences. Remember, though you will become good at noticing shifts and changes, you won't always be certain about the source or target of those changes. In other words, don't jump to conclusions as to what the changes mean.

EXERCISE
Observing Changes in Your Partner's Face

Sit opposite each other and relax your bodies. If your body is tense, you will lose your capacity to notice details. If you're overly aware of yourself during this exercise, the same problem will occur. Focus *outward* only, except to occasionally sweep your body for areas of tension. Simply let those tensions go as soon as possible and as best as possible. Keep your attention focused outward on your object of "meditation," which is your partner's face.

You're going to pay special attention to all shifts and changes you see in your partner's:

- facial muscles

- facial color

- eye movements

- pupil dilation and constriction

- head movements

When noticing facial muscles, look for tightening or loosening of skin and muscles around the neck as well as lower, middle, and upper sections of the face. Don't forget to notice upper and lower eyelids. Look for controls on the face, times when your partner's face is too still or frozen in place. Is their smile fluid or controlled?

Color changes in the skin due to blood flow. With some folks, color really changes strongly in the neck and face as their arousal goes up or down.

Notice small changes in the eyes; how they move or don't move. When do the pupils shift?

Now, with each shift or change you notice, I want you to use your index finger to gently tap your thigh. If you notice a slight tightening in their forehead . . . tap. Your partner shifts their eyes up, down, left, or right . . . tap. Their pupils dilate a bit . . . tap. Your partner smiles slightly . . . tap. With any and all changes you *think* you see . . . tap. You can both do this at the same time or you can alternate. You can do this when you're out to dinner without announcing what you're doing. Just practice. You can practice with other people as well. Nobody has to know that you're tapping "change" on your thigh. Right?

The first step toward reading faces is noticing tiny shifts and changes. Don't interpret. Don't read into these changes. Just start by attending to shifts. You can also observe people in close-up on television.

LEARNING YOUR PARTNER BY OBSERVATION

Now that you're armed with some information on your partner's facial tells, you're going to use this new skill to get even more information about your partner. This is the process by which you will become an expert on your mate and vice versa. Don't simply rely on what your partner says or your knee-jerk reactions to what you think your partner is telling you. Really pay attention, as if you don't know what you think you know. Make sense? Let's give it a try.

Becoming an Expert on Your Partner

Getting to know your partner, discovering who they are in all their strengths and quirks, is *fun*. It's also fun to be discovered. So use the quiz below as your version of *The Newlywed Game*, only on steroids.

Rules

Sit directly across from each other, in close proximity, either on the floor or in chairs. Start off with a period of silent gazing into each other's eyes. It's important to remain silent for at least two to five minutes. Make sure your faces are well lit so that you can see each other's pupils.

Partner A reads a question aloud to partner B. (See question examples below.) Partner B responds and partner A must determine if partner B's response is true or false by examining the partner's face during and after they speak by saying "hot," "warm," or "cold."

Question Example: What scares you the most, from early childhood to this day? You want to know your partner's greatest fear. How are you going to find out? You could ask, but the answer may not be correct. Why? Because we make things up based on memory. To discover what's true, you're going to sherlock your partner, meaning you're going to watch, wait, and wonder what they'll do in response to your guess.

Procedure

After you read the question aloud, remain quiet and examine your partner's face. While studying your partners eyes, give your answer, *just one*, so you can measure your partner's response. IMPORTANT: Keep your answer pithy, to the point, and without phrasing it as a question.

- After making your guess, wait and watch carefully.

- Pay special attention to your partner's facial cues, noticing any changes in the color of their skin and eyes (movement, pupil size, watering); in the lower part of the face; and body posture.

- Ask yourself if you're hot, warm, or cold with your guess.

- Then ask your partner: "Am I hot, warm, or cold?"

- Judge if your guess hits the target by watching your partner's response. If you're unsure, repeat your answer and pay close attention.

No other information should be given, by the way. We're looking for a bull's-eye and nothing less. Work to find the correct answer. Don't become disheartened if you get it wrong. Your partner will appreciate that you're curious and willing to try again.

Here are some other questions to ask and guess the answer to. I want you to get good at reading your partner's face. The more you do this, the better you will get at it.

- What's your partner's favorite thing to do?

- What's your partner's least favorite thing to do?

- What scares your partner the most from childhood?

- What are the signs and symptoms that your partner is afflicted with this fear?
    - ~ How would you minister to them?

- What's your partner's kryptonite? That experience that would knock your partner for a loop or disable them?
    - ~ What are the signs and symptoms that your partner is afflicted by this?
    - ~ How would you minister to them?

- What makes your partner cry? Movies? Plays? Music? Art? What are the themes and triggers?

- What's your partner's favorite music?

- What's your partner's favorite food?

- What about you annoys your partner?

- What makes you a difficult partner in your partner's mind?

- What do you need to learn?

- What triggers your partner's anger?

- What calms your partner down?

- Does your partner think you're good at calming them down?

- Does your partner believe that you tell them everything?

- Does your partner believe you're truthful?

- Does your partner trust you with their life?

- Does your partner believe you would protect them?

- Do you believe your partner is hiding anything from you?

Your partner can't be all-knowing; therefore, your job of paying attention, being present, and being curious is never done. Secure-functioning partners make it a career of getting to know each other. It doesn't end. You and your partner are moving through time. You're both changing. Are you keeping up? Do you know who's important and not important in your partner's social life? Do you know their current issues at work or school? Do you know what your partner thinks about at night? Or during lovemaking? Do you know what makes your partner feel absolutely loved? Do you know the things your partner needs to hear from you—their primary attachment figure—for the rest of their lives?

Getting facts about your partner incorrect or even slightly incorrect can not only become an irritant but can also be downright threatening. Why? Because you're supposed to know these things. If you keep telling your partner something flattering and it's not what your partner *needs* to hear, why are you saying it? Have you been paying attention?

Marie and Jim are about to celebrate Marie's fortieth birthday. Jim loves Marie, but he's a bit lunkheaded when it comes to gifts. Marie sent him pictures of a white Mini Cooper convertible with a red top, which she's wanted for a long time. Jim ignores her hints and buys her a brown Mercedes Benz sedan. Imagine his face when she registers the news with disappointment. She couldn't have been clearer, but he didn't pay attention. "What's the difference?" he complained. "This is a better car." Jim didn't understand.

Your partner *is not you*. Know the animal you're with. Know how they tick. Become an expert in your partner. Be your partner's whisperer. You and your partner will never regret it.

7

DEAL BREAKERS

There are very real obstacles to secure functioning, which I call deal breakers. A deal breaker is any matter that would disqualify a partner from a committed relationship despite other wonderful conditions. It's a no-go, nonnegotiable issue that, if not fully taken off the table, exists as a cancer in your relationship. Because human beings loathe to lose the potential for everlasting love, partners may be prone to overlook, defer, or bend reality to avoid a deal breaker. Yet you will inevitably have to reckon with these issues. These avoided deal breakers threaten the relationship by their mere existence and can cause unintended and seemingly unrelated conflicts when couples avoid the "elephant in the room." Either way, deal breakers will eventually "get" the couple.

Common deal breakers involve having children, monogamy, religion, money, sex, drugs and alcohol, child-rearing, place of residence (city versus countryside), and management of thirds (children, exes, pets, hobbies, addictions, and so forth). A deal breaker for one couple might not be one for another. For instance, both partners may agree to an open marriage or one partner may have sole control of the finances. Secure functioning is about mutual agreements that serve a mutual good. You can learn to work around differences and find ways to create a secure attachment with each other. Still, it's important to get everything out in the open to save lots of suffering in the long run.

Pay attention to deal breakers! Don't just kick the can down the road and expect that deal breakers will take care of themselves. Secure-functioning partners are comfortable with reality. They're brave enough to face it straight on, instead of bending it to avoid fears and loss. I don't want to see you in my office because you decided to look the other way, swept deal breakers under the carpet, or sacrificed your own healthy self-entitlement to an insecure-functioning relationship. So put everything out on the table.

I'VE ALWAYS WANTED CHILDREN

Of all the big deal breakers, differences between partners about having or not having children is perhaps the biggest. The desire for children is highly complex and can't simply be reduced to biology. The need to raise children is felt regardless of gender identity, sexual orientation, personality, and even age. Some people are dead set against having children. Others are neutral. Still others want and have wanted children ever since childhood. It's as hot a topic today as it's been throughout the millennia. If one of you wants children and the other doesn't, it's time to have that sit-down and take this deal breaker off the table! Yet one of you may be less than certain that you *don't* want children. You could be convinced. That's different, so continue with the sit down! Remember that half of all pregnancies are unplanned so . . . plan for that.

I've met many individuals and couples whose main reason for a committed partnership is to have children. If this is your primary reason for pair-bonding, make sure your partner is in it for the exact same reason—and that you've discussed your desires around family in depth.

Take a page from Perry and Martha's experience. After ten years of marriage both complained of a lack of passion. Martha's dream from childhood was to have a little girl. (She even chose a name for the child during her own childhood.) Perry always dreamed of having a child too. Neither had ever carried dreams of finding love in partnership. So why were they complaining of no passion, since neither sought this out? Once we clarified why they really got together, the passion issue was no longer relevant. Being good parents was the only theme that fit with their personal goals. Once they both understood that their highest priority for their marriage was to have children, they were able to relax the pressure to have a passionate marriage.

Differences in desires for family are often difficult to resolve, which is why, when you're considering long-term partnership, it's so important to dig deep into this topic before marriage.

Take Teresa and Marla. Teresa always wanted to be a mother. Not so with Marla, who dreamed of a loving, committed relationship with a woman who wanted a childless relationship, but she accepted the deal anyway. Enter the child. Teresa became consumed by her devotion to their child, leaving Marla without a satisfying adult relationship. The rather late revelation of their differences led to a deal breaker where Marla ended the relationship.

How Do You Feel about Children?

Have a serious, in-depth conversation about bringing children into your relationship:

- Are the two of you a secure-functioning couple, inviting a child to join your party?

- What purpose would be served from bringing a child into your relationship?

- What does each of you see as the highest priority: your child or your partner relationship?

Be sure neither of you is dodging, avoiding, complying, short-changing, or cutting corners on this issue. Don't wait for the child to come into your life before you realize this is a deal breaker.

If you both agree *not* to have children, great. You can be terrific with other people's children, and you don't have to take them home with you. Rent them instead. However, if the two of you are on the same page with regard to having children, there are some things you should consider.

Your Lives Will Change Forever

Secure-functioning partners understand the importance of being and staying informed. Ask your friends with children how their lives changed. Really interview them. Find out what you can expect, such as lack of sleep, tabling date night for a while, a reduced sex life perhaps due to a change of libido (or due to exhaustion, infatuation, and preoccupation with the newborn).

One thing is for sure, you will never feel the same about yourself or your relationship, and that isn't meant to be negative. Having a child can increase your love and affection for each other and your joint sense of purpose in life. It's a game changer to be sure. And . . . it's forever. If you're having and raising children together, remember it is a *couple endeavor*, not an individual one (unless of course you are a single parent). Hopefully you won't have children unless your relationship is secure functioning. You're both happy as little clams with your partnership and now you would like to invite someone else to the party. That means you will be thoughtful about what you're about to do, planning early how to go about it. I don't mean what color to paint the baby's room but rather division of labor, who is doing what and how you will help each other. As the two of you prepare to add another person to your family, it's important that both of you are fully resourced with money, time, help, support, comfort, food, sleep, and so on.

MY PARTNER HAS CHILDREN, AND I'M READY TO HAVE A FAMILY

Dive in! But beware. If you're childless and entering a readymade family, you may find yourself in over your head if the two of you don't research the pitfalls of stepparenting—and make sure you're on the same page in terms of what becoming a blended family will look like for you. You should be asking yourselves the same questions mentioned in the section above and considering the added challenges and joys of entering a stepfamily configuration. It's all too common for the couple to have a beautiful connection and ignore the questions that arise when you blend families. The ages of the children matter, and so do their genders. Also important is the current relationship with the nonresiding biological parent. The best possible situation is where all parents get along and work cooperatively and collaboratively to make child-rearing as easy as possible.

Nicolette and Martin are thirty-four and forty-five, respectively, and are getting married. Both have been married twice before. Nicolette is a very independent woman with her own lingerie company. She's childless. Martin has two daughters from his prior marriage. Though together for over a year, Nicolette has yet to meet Martin's children. This is troubling to her.

Martin	My daughters have been through a lot with my divorce. Their mother is very angry with me and doesn't want the girls anywhere they can be hurt again. I understand this. They'll be a part of our lives, but we just have to go very slowly.
Nicolette	Martin! We've been together for long enough and we're getting married in six months. This isn't normal. How much longer do you think this should wait? I'm already becoming demonized by your ex, and the girls are saying things about me—really unflattering things.
Martin	They haven't said anything negative about you. They track me online and see pictures of us together. They're judging me, not you. They see your online catalog with you sometimes modeling lingerie and they're judgy.
Me	What exactly is the problem with the girls meeting Nicolette?
Martin	I just don't want to traumatize them any more than I have.
Me	How have they been traumatized exactly?
Martin	Just the divorce. It was hard on them because my ex-wife started drinking a lot right after the separation and threatened to hurt herself. The girls had to deal with my leaving and with a mother who was spiraling out of control.

Me	Do you expect Nicolette will be a good stepmother?
Martin	[long pause] I think they will like her, yes.
Me	That's not what I asked.
Martin	I think Nic could be a lot of fun for them. Nic is very outgoing and young at heart. And she's very independent, not like their mother. I think she'll be a good influence.
Nicolette	You don't really believe I'll be a good stepmother, do you? I'm not hearing that you do.
Martin	Well, you've never had kids and as far as I know, never wanted them. I think . . . oh jeez, I don't really want to go here.
Nicolette	If you felt this way, why didn't you say anything before? I told you that I would really like to play a parental role with your girls. Many times. You've said nothing other than, "That's so great."
Martin	It *is* great. It's just that . . . you're not the mother type. You know that. You're not that person.

Dos and Don'ts Regarding Blended Families

- DO learn about stepfamilies ahead of time.

- DO put your relationship, hierarchically, at the top of the food chain. That doesn't mean you will neglect the children or other vital interests, but that the couple understands their station as leaders, governors, and ambassadors to each of the children as well as the other parent figures and family of origin members. New partners share the joy, pain, and challenges of properly managing each other first, and everyone else second.

- DO understand and respect that stepchildren have an allegiance to biological parents and siblings.

- DO seek professional help as you would in premarital counseling to prepare for being a stepfamily.

- DO cooperate and collaborate to maintain the same attitude when dealing with ex-partners who are parents *and* each of the children.

- DO know that children's attitudes toward losing a biological parent and gaining a stepparent change as their brains develop and evolve. It's normal for a small child (three to five years old) to accept a new parent easily and then become unaccepting at another critical period of development. Work together as partners to help reassure and soothe each other whenever important relationships become conflicted.

- DON'T allow stepchildren to divide the primary attachment system, which is the couple.

- DON'T be unprepared for secure functioning.

- DON'T pretend to be a biological parent. Don't take on the role of disciplinarian until the time comes when you've earned that right with each stepchild.

- DON'T expect or allow your partner to discipline your biological child. Parent as a team, where much of your teamwork is done backstage and not in front of the kids.

- DON'T let ex-spouses cause mayhem. Keep your focus on the new couple, not the old, instead of letting an angry or vengeful ex take center stage.

- DON'T use the children as bait or leverage with each other or your ex-partners. Don't try to control the ex-partner's parenting. If the two of you couldn't agree on parenting when you were married, you certainly aren't going to improve on this when divorced or separated. If anything, you will have even less control and influence.

Today, blended families are the norm, and the challenges that arise while raising a blended family aren't really that different from other kinds of challenges a couple will face. If partners start off as secure functioning, managing a blended family should work out just fine.

THE MATTER OF MONOGAMY

Consider Tori and Gus. Gus, thrice married and thrice divorced, was twenty years older than Tori, who had never been married. When she met Gus, she believed she'd found the man she'd been waiting for. Gus also felt "she was the one." Thus far, Gus had lived life freely and unencumbered by monogamy. He expected this would continue throughout his life. Tori, on the other hand, came from a more traditional background and wasn't interested in polyamory, for either of them. From the start, Gus was completely open about his desires and very firm about what he wanted. This was clearly a bad deal for Tori, whose principles of monogamy and equality didn't fit Gus's picture of marriage. But she wanted to be married and therefore went ahead with the nuptials. Would she ever be happy in an open marriage? Extremely doubtful. What about Gus? Would he rue the day he married Tori because she wasn't in tune with his principles and lifestyle? If she continued to be unhappy, yes.

FIDELITY

The term *fidelity* is defined by the Oxford Dictionary as "faithfulness to a person, cause, or belief, demonstrated by continuing loyalty and support." We often view fidelity as synonymous with monogamy. Yet the term has a much broader meaning. Infidelity and betrayal, therefore, shouldn't be limited to cheating either sexually or romantically on your partner.

THE MATTER OF RELIGION

Robert and Jessica, both in their early thirties, were of two different religions. Robert, a conservative Jewish man from an Orthodox Jewish family, asserted his feelings that Jessica, a not-so-religious Jewish woman from an agnostic Jewish family, respect his Jewish traditions, keep a kosher house, and observe the Jewish Sabbath every week. The two were in love and engaged to be married. Robert wanted to return to Jewish orthodoxy and become a rabbi. Jessica wanted the freedoms of a modern Jewish woman. This was a matter of increasing tensions between the two of them. Neither wanted to lose the other and tried to reconcile their differences. In the end, Robert broke off the engagement.

THE MATTER OF MONEY

Money can be a deal breaker. For example, if one person comes to the table with money and the other without, trouble can develop when deciding on buying a house, sharing expenses, or setting up a joint bank account. While these issues themselves might not be deal breakers, this kind of disparity can lead to one.

I often meet couples who signed prenuptial agreements and have problems with money after marriage. Osmen and Damla, a young Turkish couple, both in their midthirties, agreed to a prenup shortly before the wedding. Though they considered each other Americanized and modern compared to their parents, and had planned to marry without a prenup, after his father's prompting Osmen asked for a prenup and Damla agreed to sign it. The wedding was imminent, and she felt she had no choice, even though the prenup clearly stated that she had no rights to Osmen's family business or his estate until they were married for fifteen years.

Ten years into the marriage, Damla still resented her husband's last-minute demand for a prenup because it felt unjust, unfair, and paternalistic. It also served as a harbinger for other inequities to come, such as being shut out of any and all of Osmen's family meetings. Hers is an example of a deal breaker deferred. Both partners suffered because of this.

THE MATTER OF SEX

The question of sexual compatibility is a common issue in my clinic among married couples but it doesn't come up much in my premarital cases. Still, new couples can have problems in this area especially when one partner is more sexually experienced, partners are religious and waiting for marriage before becoming intimate, one or both partners have unresolved sexual trauma, or cultural differences between partners influence expectation and attitudes about sexuality. In the chapter on sex, we look into the matter of compatibility and common sexual issues that plague most couples. But here I want to keep the subject limited to deal breakers as they appear before a long-term commitment such as marriage.

Deshawn, an attorney, is planning to marry his longtime friend, Kelly, a physician. Both were previously married and divorced. They were each other's confidants throughout their marriages, becoming best friends and the go-to people for just about everything, except sex. They decided to marry some years later, but Kelly worries that she doesn't feel strong erotic feelings for Deshawn, as she has had for other men. Kelly reported her libido as always being high, whereas Deshawn claimed his was just average. Deshawn was aware of this and believed it would take care of itself naturally, although he worried about Kelly's fidelity.

Sexual chemistry is a common confusion among partners who began as good friends. Because most couples go through a courtship phase where they're relatively novel to each other, their relationship is more likely to be jet-fueled by stimulating neurochemicals, such as dopamine and noradrenaline, as well as testosterone and phenylethylamine. As this love potion for newbie partners fades, partners move out of infatuation. Deshawn and Kelly never went through this phase and thus believe there may be a problem. After all, they skipped that initial euphoric novelty stage. Is that really a problem? And is this a deal breaker?

Well, there's more. Kelly says she needs sex far more frequently than Deshawn. He'd be happy having sex once or twice a week whereas Kelly wants sex daily. Now we might be edging more toward a deal breaker. Kelly likes an aggressive man during sex. Deshawn, while not a passive man, isn't exactly what Kelly prefers. He likes foreplay while Kelly enjoys being taken without much fuss.

The couple debated these and other issues around sex for a long time after they married. Their sexual appetites changed and their attitudes around lovemaking matured into something deeper and more meaningful than their previously held ideas about sex. Their intense focus on sex drove them to greater understanding about themselves. In other words, they resolved what could have been a deal breaker as they came to a sexual congress with each other (no pun intended). (See chapter 8 for more on sex.)

THE MATTER OF DRUGS AND ALCOHOL

Let me start off by saying that addiction can be a serious mental and physical health issue. When someone is in the throes of an addiction, either with a substance or behavioral addiction, every aspect of the relationship will deteriorate. Having said that, addiction is a psycho-biological issue that encompasses far more than simply genetics, family history, and the brain's reward circuit. It's also a relationship matter, a regulation matter, and an attachment matter.

Many couples have disagreements about the use of drugs and alcohol. When a couple finds themselves at a crossroads on these matters, they tend to sweep these issues under the rug, believing that one or the other will come around to their position. But this rarely happens. Of course, some couples enjoy using drugs and alcohol together, and others are fine with one person partaking without the other, and therefore they don't have a problem.

Though many partners will complain about addictions for various reasons, the one that's likely to become a secure-functioning issue is the matter of unavailability—physically, mentally, and/or emotionally. The most common complaint about substance use is the change in behavior, attitude, engagement, and alertness in the partner who is using drugs or alcohol. A partner who is altered can be not only obnoxious and unattractive but also hostile, aggressive, and even violent. Acts of violence are commonly perpetrated by an alcohol-drenched brain. That alone should be a deal breaker. Still, even a stoned, drunk, or tripping partner is a drag if the other partner is sober, not interested, and unhappy with their altered lover. Repeat that experience, and you have abandonment and neglect problems.

But what of the partners who enjoy smoking pot together? No problem so far as secure functioning is concerned. How about drinking, using porn, binge-watching television, or any other activity that's ordinarily autoregulatory? As long as it's interactive and the partners are engaged, no problem. I've had barfly couples in my clinic.* Those are alcoholic or drug-abusing couples who appear in complete accord with their lifestyle. Now, I worried about the safety of these folks, but I didn't focus on this in therapy unless their substance abuse became relevant to the problems they were facing as a couple.

There are, of course, situations wherein substance or behavioral addictions (pornography, sex, food, and so forth) become a deal breaker, as in the example below.

Sam and Sherry, together since their teens, both enjoyed partying and drug use. It wasn't until they decided to marry and have children that Sherry started to complain. She decided to become sober in preparation for building a family and expected Sam to do the same. Sam believed this was an unfair and unexpected change in their relationship. He lobbied hard to continue his drug and alcohol use. While Sherry initially just complained about his continuing substance abuse, she eventually put her foot down. Sam sobered up. A week into their marriage she discovered that he was still using and hiding it from her. She was furious and felt betrayed by him. The deal breaker that she thought had been taken off the table had remained a deal breaker. After several months, she decided to file for divorce.

BETRAYALS AND WITHHOLDING
VITAL INFORMATION

Secure-functioning relationships start with partners accepting each other as is and end with absolute protection of the couple's safety and security system. Mutual trust is part of that foundation. Partners must be able to trust each other when they share information about others, including parents, children, friends, and associates. Misinformation,

---

* *Barfly* was an semiautobiographical book and film about Charles Bukowski and his experiences as a barfly, along with his equally alcoholic partner.

falsehoods, omissions, frequent use of deception, or lying will destroy trust in an interdependent relationship where the primary reason for existing is based on trust. In their wonderful book *Tell Me No Lies*, Ellyn Bader and Peter T. Pearson talk about the difference between constructive lies and ones that will destroy your relationship.[1]

A particularly dangerous form of deception, the one I focus on in this book, is exceptionally devastating. Revealing previously unknown vital information has a jarring and oftentimes deeply disturbing effect on the recipient of such knowledge. It forces that person to reevaluate everything from the beginning of the relationship because, if previously known, it may have changed everything, including whether the relationship would exist at all.

Many partners make the mistake of withholding important information such as sexually transmitted diseases, trauma histories, abuse histories, previous marriages, previous sexual behavior that might affect the other partner, critical financial info, and so forth. There are partners who misrepresent facts such as their real age, religious preferences, financial status, family of origin status, medical conditions, or other vital information. The longer information is withheld or misrepresented, the greater the risk that the partner who had been in the dark will feel betrayed. This is compounded if the information is discovered rather than offered voluntarily—worse still if information was concealed with lying or intent to deceive.

Candace and Jenny were engaged and living together on the eastern coast of the United States. In the weeks leading up to the wedding, Jenny stumbled upon information about Candace's past relationships, including that she was previously married to a male partner. Jenny was stunned and disoriented, and confronted Candace hoping to hear it was untrue. Candace tried desperately to explain why she withheld the information, but Jenny was so upset she spent the night at her parents' home. Candace was able to console Jenny and plans for the wedding continued.

Shortly thereafter, Jenny again stumbled upon more unknown information when she happened to look at Candace's driver's license. It indicated that her birth date was different by eight years (older) than what she had told Jenny. When confronted, Candace again apologized for the misinformation, stating that she was simply afraid that Jenny would reject her if she knew her real age. Jenny promptly ended the relationship. She felt betrayed by Candace's lack of transparency and believed the broken trust amounted to a deal breaker going forward.

I could go on and on with examples of revelations of previously unknown vital information. It's never a good idea to withhold, conceal, or misrepresent information vital to the other partner's interests, and it never ends well. Please take heed. If you have left out important information your partner should know, even if you think it may be unimportant, don't delay. The longer it takes for you to tell your partner, the more likely it will be experienced as a betrayal. If you're edging toward a commitment with your partner, don't be passive or fear being intrusive or nosy. You're going to be in the foxhole together with this person. You need to know everything you can before putting yourself in that position. You have a right to know who you're going to trust with your life, as does your partner.

Some betrayals have longer memories than others. For instance, there are mini betrayals when one partner fails to uphold a mutually shared principle of governance, such as failing to share information about a current situation, withholding relatively nonessential information that might cause your partner to be angry, or revealing information publicly that the other partner wants to remain private. These things happen and only become a big problem when the offending partner becomes defensive, dismissive, or remains insensitive to their partner's feelings.

However, when partners are in a precommitment or premarital phase and one fails to protect the other from a family member, friend, or ex-partner, this can be a betrayal that can remain in memory for a very long time. Of course, breaches of trust, failures to protect, and issues with thirds will always be a problem if the offending partner fails to see the errors of their ways and doesn't swiftly course-correct. I've seen many a union suffer from an early history where a partner was thrown under the bus in favor of someone or something else. It's a betrayal that demonstrates treason in the eyes of the betrayed partner. If not repaired and corrected immediately, it can pose an enduring threat to the safety and security system for many years to come.

Discoveries of previously undisclosed vital information can represent both a betrayal and a deal breaker, depending upon the information revealed. If the information given or discovered represents values that are diametrically opposed to the values of the other partner, then it could be a deal breaker. If the betrayal involved lying, gaslighting (making someone question their reality), or the flagrant use of deception, the betrayal may be too great for the relationship to move forward.

MISMANAGEMENT OF THIRDS REDUX

A few deal breakers have to do with the management of thirds. One partner may believe that their work is the absolute biggest priority in their life, whereas the other partner believes that their children should come first and that work should always take a back seat to family time. Thirds are in-laws, children, stepchildren, ex-spouses, drugs and alcohol, hobbies, porn—anything that could take the focus off ensuring the integrity of your couple bubble. Mismanagement of thirds will injure at least one partner, but chronic mismanagement can and often does destroy the relationship because it's experienced as a betrayal. As a therapist, I don't take a stand on who or what should come first. Partners must agree on these things. And each partner should be careful that they aren't giving up a significant life need or desire in making agreements. The story below is an example of how Tracey and I managed our relationship with her (then) ten-year-old daughter, Joanna.

My Story

Tracey will often say to people that I married her along with her child, three cats, a dog, and an ex-husband. When it came to Joanna, I was fearful of becoming attached to a child who could fire me, because I'm not blood. I was the intruder, the one who posed a threat to her relationship with her mother. This was compounded because Joanna had had her mother to herself for many years. Tracey and I had to decide how to manage this threesome.

From the beginning, Joanna and I struggled as I learned to be a proper stepparent. Tracey wanted to protect Joanna from feeling left out or pushed out by our new relationship. I can't say that forging a relationship with Joanna was easy. But it was all worth it. We would fight and then make up. I would admit my feelings (and my missteps) while learning how to be a stepparent. Losing my temper was easier than making amends, but with time, I became better at both. While there was some skill involved in overcoming the hurdle of becoming part of a blended family, there was also a lot of luck. Joanna's real father and I get along very well. There's no more acrimony between Tracey and her ex-husband. Joanna now has two loving fathers.

It wasn't until our engagement when we asked Joanna to be part of the planning that she changed her attitude. From that point on, things changed in a major way simply because she was invited to be part of the wedding. We married with friends and family, and with my goddaughter and Joanna giving us away. Now I consider Joanna my daughter, and we're very close. But I still introduce her as my stepdaughter, respectfully, so she can honor her real father.

I feel very blessed to have gained a lifelong relationship that matters so much to me. Despite my fortune, I understand what can go wrong in blended families. I often wish more people would go into premarital counseling, and I feel that anyone who is about to become a stepparent should consider counseling. Biological parents would also benefit from this education, since the actions of both the stepparent and the biological parent can either help or hinder the process of blending families.

Deal breakers often lie hidden because partners refuse to address, acknowledge, and solve them prior to getting married. It's imperative to identify any during the premarital phase, even if they spell the potential end of the relationship. Deal breakers are ticking time bombs, which can cause a lot of pain to the couple and their children and stepchildren. Be sure to reread this chapter if necessary. The warning signs must be approached with eyes wide open and mind fully fixed on reality, if secure functioning is what you want.

8

SEX!

Physical intimacy and closeness are two of the sweetest things in life. And giving and receiving pleasure strengthens your couple bubble. Of all the pleasures afforded us by nature, sex is extolled by just about every adult on the planet. Of course, much of this is due to the phenomena of neuromuscular euphoria (a.k.a. orgasm).

Why is sex awesome? Let me count the ways. Sex:

- builds trust and intimacy

- helps heal old emotional and sexual injuries

- helps you become an expert on your partner

- helps you learn about yourself

- supports good health

- supports a healthy immune system

- improves sleep

- reduces anxiety

- decreases physical pain (not related to sex)

- leads to wanting more sex

Yet of all the common topics that people I counsel complain about—money, time, mess, sex, and kids—sex is probably the most common problem area of all. As a professional, I don't believe I'm alone in this claim.

Of all the sensory regulators—touch, taste, smell, sound, and vision—nothing compares to *touch* when it comes to effective management of the human neuroendocrine stress system. It can facilitate stress reduction better and faster than eye contact or vocal tone. We're so touch oriented that, if stressed, we might seek physical comfort ahead of other needs.* This isn't to say that friendly eye contact doesn't reduce stress. It does. However, a good hug or embrace can have more immediate downregulating effects on the autonomic nervous system and body.

WHAT IS SEX?

I'm not going to get into the birds and the bees with you here. But I do want to briefly examine our definition of the word *sex* since there doesn't appear to be just one meaning. For a great many people, sex is synonymous with traditional sexual intercourse. But even the concept of intercourse is complex and can mean different things for different couples. A young premarital couple once came to me and said they were saving themselves for marriage. They later revealed that they had anal sex but didn't consider that as going against their chastity vows.

I broadly define sex as having any erotic physical contact with another person. That would include erotic kissing, touching, and exploring, as well as vaginal intercourse, anal sex, and oral sex, with or without orgasm. This matches Merriam-Webster's definition: "Physical activity in which people touch each other's bodies, kiss each other, etc.; physical activity that is related to and often includes sexual intercourse."

---

*Mileage may vary for some islands and individuals with unresolved trauma histories. Some people are touch averse and that can be a problem in terms of stress reduction and physical and mental health.

How Do You Define Sex?

How do you define sex? Is it the same as lovemaking? What's the difference? Talk about this together. See what you come up with. I've seen some partners who consider flirting a form of sexual behavior.

WHY HAVE SEX?

Silly question? It actually isn't. Just like the reasons we marry can vary, the reasons we have sex can be quite different between partners. None of these reasons are intrinsically right or wrong. For example, just as some couples marry to have children, some may seek sex purely for procreation purposes. Regardless, sex is a natural part of what we do as partners in a romantic relationship. We've established that lovemaking is much more than coitus. It's about affection, friendship, and deepening our knowledge of each other. It's also about healing.

Imagine your physician, as part of your physical, gave you a prescription for an orgasm a day. Would you think that strange? Of course you would. But what if your physician listed all the medical benefits of such a prescription?

- reduced depression and anxiety

- reduced restless leg syndrome

- reduced physical pain by about 50 percent

- increased levels of oxytocin and vasopressin

- increased friendliness, closeness, and feelings of love and affection

- increased dopamine levels

- improved sleep

At the very least, an orgasm is better than a poke in the eye. If your physician gave you a prescription for two orgasms and a call in the morning, you would just tell your partner that it's medically imperative for you to have two orgasms tonight. No real muss or fuss.

Benefits, Benefits, Benefits

Sexual intimacy benefits both partners in many ways. One well-known benefit is the production of oxytocin and vasopressin, particularly in the female when reaching orgasm. But it's not only she who benefits from an orgasm, as males also produce oxytocin and vasopressin during and after sex. Males can produce oxytocin while in the presence of a female who is having an orgasm. A female may produce oxytocin in the presence of a male who is having an orgasm. Face-to-face and skin-to-skin contact can evoke sustained feelings of closeness and intimacy between partners. Moments such as these strengthen the safety and security system or restore safety and security when threatened. Couples often use sex to scaffold their safety and security system. However, sustained face-to-face, skin-to-skin contact can often accomplish the same thing. Moments of intimacy become especially important during transitions such as separation and reunion, prior to sleeping at night, and upon waking in the morning.

Sex is perhaps best when it's about making, generating, and sustaining feelings of love and affection. Lovemaking should be fun, but it ceases to be when it becomes overly self-conscious. Like everything else, lovemaking is about collaboration, play, exploration, discovery, healing, helping each other out, and learning about each other. Using a loving gaze, texting words of admiration and appreciation, admitting when one is wrong, pillow talk before sleep, and physical closeness also strengthen feelings of love and connection.

Sex for Pregnancy

Let's say your goal is to become pregnant. How wonderful! Many couples sail through this task because both partners are fertile and will likely have little trouble getting pregnant. Generally speaking, more than eight in ten couples having regular sex (every two to three days) will likely conceive within one year if the female is younger than forty years of age. Of those couples who don't conceive in the first year, about half will do so in the second year. Fears of becoming pregnant can complicate sexual satisfaction, especially if there isn't clear communication and responsible behavior on behalf of both partners. Nonetheless, one or both partners may continue to feel anxious about pregnancy if one or both don't want children. This issue can put strain on the couple's relationship, and not just in the bedroom.

Jim complained of erectile dysfunction and delayed orgasm with Wendy, who wanted to get pregnant. He feared that she might "accidentally" fail to take her birth control pills. He even worried about condom failure. This anxiety got in the way of their lovemaking and eventually became a real problem.

Other couples aren't as fortunate with pregnancy. Fertility issues are complex and can greatly stress a couple. Approximately one in seven couples run into various problems when conceiving. Couples can remain in limbo for months and years without seeing results. Not only do prolonged issues of infertility place stress on the couple, but they will likely also affect the couple's sex life. For these couples, sex often becomes a chore, something that pairs lovemaking with sadness, depression, anger, anxiety, and disappointment. To make matters worse, the stress encountered in these instances can itself be a complicating factor in conception. Partners who don't have a secure-functioning relationship will be at greater risk for significant marital problems if infertility is center stage.

Sexual issues involved in making babies can lead to many problems, especially for insecure-functioning couples. I've seen far too many partners come to the clinic who view sex as a baby-making enterprise.

Dos and Don'ts Regarding Having Children

- DO come to an agreement as to what comes first,
  the couple relationship or having children.

- DO become a secure-functioning couple before adding
  a third (baby).

- DO take all deal breakers off the table before having children.

- DO plan responsibly before conceiving a child. Make certain that finances, employment, and other resources are in place. Discuss role expectations in advance and come to clear agreements.

- DO consider the complexities of having a child even if you already share stepchildren.

- DON'T jump into child-rearing blindly or impulsively. Think, discuss, and plan for all possible outcomes.

- DON'T bring a child into this world if your couple relationship sucks. Many couples think that having a baby will fix their marital problems. This is rarely the case.

- DON'T allow yourselves to be underresourced before, during, and after pregnancy.

- DON'T be irresponsible or reckless when sexually active with your partner if making babies isn't your aim. Many lives are at stake.

TALKING ABOUT SEX

I'm always intrigued by the fact that so many couples don't talk about sex. Partners who are secure functioning should be able to talk about anything. That's part of the We Do agreement. I'll typically hear things such as "It isn't sexy to talk about sex," "It bogs things down," or "It's embarrassing." Yet lovemaking, as already mentioned, should be about exploration, experience, playfulness, and curiosity. If lovemaking is to deepen your knowledge and understanding of each other and yourselves, why not talk about sex even during sex? I'm not referring to defensive intentions to distract, disrupt, or deflect from the act of lovemaking. I agree, that's annoying.

Amelia came to her relationship with Greg with a sexual abuse history. She was date-raped when she was eighteen. Greg knew about this but failed to learn many details about the incident. As their relationship blossomed, Amelia's anxiety began to increase around lovemaking, and Greg mistook her hesitancy for a rejection of him personally. His behavior changed accordingly. Amelia, of course, mistook Greg's distancing as personal and linked his behavior to a comment he made to her about being out of shape. He was talking about himself, but Amelia heard it as a veiled criticism of her body. These kinds of errors increased to a level of extreme awkwardness, self-consciousness, and bitterness. Like all couples who don't talk to clarify and error-correct, these two well-meaning partners began to avoid all physical contact.

Once they began to talk about their disintegrating sex life, they discovered their failure to communicate. Within a very short period, both partners were able to straighten out their misinterpretations and learn to talk with each other during sex to help heal their injuries and uncertainties.

Problems stemming from lack of communication around sex, body image, and sensory issues abound—and they're unnecessary! I tell partners to save their money on therapy and do their jobs as secure-functioning partners. Be each other's confessors, healers, and best friends.

I've said it before and I'll say it again: real time is extremely fast, and we're mostly acting and reacting reflexively and automatically without really knowing why. Therefore, we're going to make things up in the absence of knowing, filling in the blanks with our current mind-set. We will lean toward the negative because that's what the brain tends to do. Think of all the mistakes we're going to make during lovemaking given these facts. Add our generally terrible ability to verbally communicate, and you can see why sex can be one of the most problematic areas of coupledom. But it doesn't have to be. Secure-functioning partners strive to understand each other no matter what activity they're engaged in. When you say "we do," that should include we *talk* and take care to understand each other in the most tender and vulnerable acts such as lovemaking.

TALKING DURING SEX

"Talking will ruin sex," people tell me. If talk is used to avoid intimacy, fill silences, or cover for anxiety, then yes, it will ruin a good time. I'm not referring to *that* kind of talk. Further, if a partner is feeling discomfort of any kind and keeps it to themselves, that will ruin sex as well. Same with a partner who won't admit performance anxiety in the moment, fears getting something wrong, needs to shift their position, has a sudden flashback to a bad memory or trauma, or becomes distracted, bored, or sleepy. Lovemaking includes ministering to each other, whenever necessary, and being helpful and collaborative. The understanding and expectation should be of reciprocity. Each partner gets to voice their feelings and concerns. That's part of the gig.

Dos and Don'ts Regarding Talking During Sex

- DO immediately let your partner in on thoughts or feelings that intrude on your flow.

- DO make sure your partner is totally clear on what you said or did.

- DO respond quickly to your partner's concerns, wishes, or sensitivities.

- DO be curious about your partner during sex.

- DON'T disrespect, dismiss, or devalue your partner's concerns, wishes, or sensitivities. Injuries during sex have a long memory—even longer if not repaired immediately.

- DON'T leave your actions or inactions to your partner's imagination. You won't like how their brain fills in the blanks.

- DON'T withhold information about what you're doing, thinking, feeling, or planning.

PROBLEMS THAT CAN ARISE

Most of the problems in the bedroom are fixable! First of all, they mirror problems outside of the bedroom. In the psychobiological world, partners repeat the same mistakes everywhere, regardless of the situation. In fact, if a couple's problems are focused on sex, oftentimes this makes change easier because the misunderstandings and misattunements are concentrated in one area. A great majority of sexual issues begin or worsen at common developmental milestones in the couple's history. A great many people will report problems beginning with the wedding night. Others will say that sex began to wane after a few months of dating or perhaps after moving in together. Others report that sex took a nosedive with the birth of their first child.

Let's spend time discussing what can go wrong. This is a big area in couple satisfaction and deserves some special attention.

Frequency

Couples who come into my clinic will sooner or later bring up the topic of sex, wanting to know what's "normal." They discuss the kinds of sex they're having, what makes them comfortable versus uncomfortable, and what excites them. They also wonder about frequency, timing, and the dynamics and roles that each partner plays. Underlying these complaints are the core issues: lack of connection, lack of (the feeling of) safety, lack of tenderness, and a lack of sensitivity.

Part of wondering what's normal has to do with how our culture portrays sex and sexuality, and all the confusing and even incorrect messages we receive around sex, from a young age into adulthood. Sex is a national (and international) obsession. Sex is often used in advertising, even when it has nothing to do with the product because—let's face it—sex is appealing. Books and magazine articles tell us how to have sex, how much sex to have, when to have sex, where to have sex, how long sex should last, and even what to do before, during, and after sex. It's no wonder people focus so much on their sex life. Yet with all this advice and the frequency with which people obsess over it, many of us aren't well informed or sexually masterful.

Every few years a study will come out about how much sex and what kind of sex the average American has over the course of a week, month, or year. It comes as no surprise that many couples coming to therapy worry that their sexual activity is either below or above "normal." In point of fact, a problem doesn't exist if partners are well matched in terms of their libido.

Marion We don't have enough sex.

Me What do you mean? Enough for whom?

Marion I don't know. I think we should be having more sex.

Me Do you agree with her?

Bobby Yeah, I guess so.

Me [to Marion] Are you craving sex?

Marion No, not really. [Bobby shakes his head in agreement.]

Me So you guys aren't craving more sex, but you think you should be having it. Do I have that right? [They both nod yes.] Well, if you're not craving it, where are you getting this idea that you should be having more sex? [They both shrug.]

In this example, both Bobby and Marion are judging their sex life according to what they read or hear from their friends, TV, and magazine articles. Why aren't they evaluating their sex life according to how *they* feel and think? Not very secure functioning.

Sexual Issues Around Biology

A common deal breaker for people involves sexual behavior and attitudes. Some partners don't want their partner to masturbate, look at pornography, look at the opposite sex, and so on. Other people will break up because their partner isn't exciting, experimental, or sensual enough. Others still want to open the marriage, swing with other couples, go to nude beaches, and engage in other activities that involve nudity and sex with strangers.

Psychobiological issues, personal preferences, and complicating factors play into our desire for sex and can lead to sexual dysfunction. Psychobiological issues are due to both medical and psychological conditions. For instance, erectile dysfunction can be due to age, medications, surgeries, and use of alcohol and street drugs, but also anxiety, depression, performance pressure, and overuse of pornography. Dyspareunia (vaginal pain especially during intercourse) can point to a medical problem but can also be aggravated by anxiety, relationship disturbances, and sexual trauma history. A medical checkup is always advised before looking at other possible causes; however, good statistics show that these problems are at least influenced by mental state. As one who studies both the brain and the body, I see reason to consider all sexual complaints within this framework of mind and body.

Secure-functioning partners will take biologically identified sexual dysfunction seriously without blame, but they will also keep an open mind to the interpersonal aspects of the problem—again, without blame.

Marta and Ben, newly married, have been having problems with intercourse, which has been very painful for Marta. She had a workup by her gynecologist and was diagnosed with vaginismus (involuntary/painful pelvic floor spasm with attempted vaginal penetration). The problem caused both she and Ben physical pain. She was referred to a pelvic floor physical therapist with whom she does exercises and has been given a dilator for both she and Ben to use for help with relaxation.

As secure-functioning partners, neither Ben nor Marta use the vaginismus diagnosis as a way to blame Marta. Ben happens to be a very large man with . . . you know . . . a larger-than-average penis. Marta is petite. Neither were experienced in sexual intercourse and both wanted to have children. While both partners tended to be quite anxious about their bodies, their ability to perform sexually, and their ability to please their partner, they used sexual exploration as a way to talk and slowly move through their fears and anxieties. In other words, they used their sexual concerns as opportunities to deepen their relationship, to minister to each other, and to heal old insecurities and fears.

If Ben and Marta were insecure functioning, the biological matter of vaginismus would have easily advanced to psychobiological problems involving threat. In the area of sex, this one-person psychological attitude will most certainly tank the relationship. We must understand that our interpersonal problems aren't about money, time, sex, mess, or kids. Nor are they about who parks where and who leaves the dishes out.

They're about how we view the couple system. Is it a two-person system with emphasis on cooperation, collaboration, and mutual respect and admiration? Is it a system that values the relationship above all else due to an interpersonal need for surviving and thriving? Remember, the test of a good couple is the amount of load bearing the system can tolerate without breaking apart. Might as well practice with sex!

Sexual Issues Around Personal Preferences

I remember Janice complaining about the words Bill used while making love to her. He liked to swear and found it a turn-on to use the f-word when they were intimate. As a teenager, before she became sexually active, Janice was told that this kind of language was reserved for sex with prostitutes, and she felt denigrated when Bill spoke to her this way. Misinterpreting sexual preferences is why sex, an area in which many of us are at our most vulnerable, can become a source of conflict and strife instead of leading to more closeness and intimacy. We have to create a safe place in which to explore, experiment, and express our love physically. We can help each other by going slowly, checking with each other, and admitting our mistakes.

Proximity Seeking and Contact Maintenance

Contact maintenance is how long I remain in physical contact with you before wanting to physically remove myself. It's how long I can remain gazing into your eyes before darting away or averting my gaze, and how long I can talk about our relationship before wanting to change the subject, move away, or check out. Proximity seeking and contact maintenance have little to do with love and a lot to do with safety and security. How we physically move toward and away from others, especially a primary attachment figure, is informed by body memory from very early childhood. Are you someone who can hold hands for a long time? How long is too long? What about a kiss? Or a hug? Check your own timing.

Tommy makes several bids for connection with Bev. He'll look over at her, take her hand into his, put his arm around her, and check in with her every so often. He likes seeking her attention and he likes physical closeness. Bev, on the other hand, doesn't seek Tommy's attention very much. She avoids eye contact and she's not nearly as affectionate as he is. It's not that she doesn't love Tommy. She does. She's not a proximity seeker—she doesn't crave sustained physical contact. When holding hands, Bev will disengage after a few minutes, which at times, hurts Tommy, mostly due to the way Bev handles her need to physically break away.

"What's wrong?" asks Tommy after Bev pulls her hand away from his.

"Nothing," she replies. "It's getting uncomfortable and sweaty." Bev says this while keeping her head facing forward and away from him, furthering Tommy's feeling of rejection.

Now you might identify with either or both Tommy and Bev in this example, and you may say to yourself, "I know what that feels like and I hate it." Nonetheless, if I told you that a small tweak of this situation would satisfy both partners, would you believe me? Here's the same situation but with a tiny adjustment: Bev, while holding Tommy's hand, kisses his hand and gently removes it with her other hand. Voilà! No hurt and no guilt. That minor change satisfies both her need to break away and his need to feel loved. Done.

<hr>

EXERCISE
Proximity Seeking

Try this with your partner: Next time you're together, count how many times you visually, vocally, and physically seek physical proximity with your partner. Have you partner count too. Compare notes after a morning, afternoon, or evening together. DON'T JUDGE.

Sexually Avoidant Partners

There's no couple activity as exposing as sex, nothing that requires as much proximity seeking and contact maintenance. Sexually avoidant partners have a difficult time tolerating intimacy, especially when it involves repeated and sustained close physical proximity within the context of a "permanent" relationship. These partners may cite a low libido when actually they can't tolerate the kind of repeated and sustained face-to-face, skin-to-skin interaction that commonly occurs during sex. Sexually avoidant partners often have a history of early childhood neglect of an interpersonal nature with the primary caregivers.

One of the common ailments of the avoidant is to retreat from sex that's interactive or mutual. Avoidant men and women commonly like to have unreciprocated oral sex, with many preferring oral sex over intercourse in general. For the avoidant, oral sex can resolve the interpersonal stress problem, as can sex with the lights off and sexual positions whereby one partner's back is to the other or one partner's face is hidden. This isn't to say that oral sex, whether reciprocated or not, is a problem, nor is having the lights off or the face hidden.

If one partner is avoidant, the other partner will likely complain of feeling rejected, although it's not personal. The avoidant's phobic reaction to dependency and coregulation preexists the relationship and is likely found in other areas of engagement. It's probable that neither partner understands this and that both misappraise the other's intentions, feelings, and behaviors. A partner who is avoidant will commonly feel ashamed in reaction to their distancing reflexes. The avoidant's partner will commonly feel undesired or unwanted.

The couple therapist can help both partners sort this out by helping each understand how avoidance originates, develops, and operates in the adult primary attachment relationship. Although one partner will appear avoidant, it's highly likely that both partners share similar avoidant tendencies, a fact that's hidden by the behavior of the more avoidant, acting-out partner. I encourage both of you to help each other acclimate to interpersonal stress without having to avoid, withdraw, dissociate, or triangulate.

EXERCISE
Contact Maintenance

Try this with your partner: Go in for a full body hug and hold it like statues. Make sure your chests and stomachs are touching. Try to notice your thoughts and body sensations, and pay special attention to when you want to end the hug. If you can, see if you can feel your partner making moves to get away. Talk to each other about your thoughts and impulses. DON'T JUDGE.

Other ways to test contact maintenance:

- sustained eye contact

- sustained talking about the relationship

- sustained hand-holding

- sustained cuddling (in or out of bed)

Performance Anxiety

Anxiety around performance is a real joy killer. Here's why. Several areas of the brain can interfere with something called *flow*, a term well known by musicians, artists, actors, dancers, and athletes. Flow is a state of consciousness whereby one is immersed in an activity, fully absorbed, with a feeling of electrified focus that's distinctly pleasurable and without self-consciousness. Flow requires a balance between skill and demand, or ability and challenge. Such a balance allows us to meet an activity without threat or loss and therefore resources are freed up for flow.

As I've said previously, during courtship or one-night stands, nature's cocktail can override problems with performance pressure and attachment insecurities for a while. Eventually we're all left with baseline issues that can interfere with flow and therefore sexual performance.

Sexual drive and interest will change throughout the lifespan for various reasons. If you expect to maintain the same libidinal energy throughout your time together you will likely be greatly disappointed. Besides, nothing kills libido like high expectations and performance pressure. Scheduling sex can be a real buzzkill, and it can make it an overly precious and therefore avoidable exercise. Resist scheduling sex.

Dos and Don'ts Regarding Performance Anxiety

- DO keep yourself relaxed but alert enough to maintain continuous focus on your partner's face, eyes, and body.

- DO keep pouring all your attention on your senses: vision, smell, touch, and taste.

- DO collaborate fully with your partner in helping them reach an orgasm.

- DON'T schedule sex.

- DON'T think!

Save your money on therapists or sex experts and stop reading magazine articles that tell you what you should be doing with each other. Become your own experts. If lovemaking is what you want, dump end goals, including orgasm. Forget about achieving anything. Just be with each other. Improvise the moment. Don't plan. Don't schedule.

Problems in the Near Senses

The near senses are smell, touch, taste, and near vision, because they occur in close proximity to another person. (Hearing isn't included.) Problems in sex can arise in these areas because of our varying degrees of sensitivity. When Caroline became pregnant, her sense of smell was heightened and suddenly she couldn't stand the smell of onion on her husband's breath. When she asked Josh to stop breathing on her, he felt affronted and insulted. Though she explained that the smell of onions made her ill, he nevertheless continued to feel hurt. His insensitivity around this complaint hurt her deeply. He liked onions and, besides, she never complained before. The more he ignored her olfactory aversion, the more she pulled away when he tried to engage in sex or just cuddle. The longer she avoided him, the more damage it did and the harder it became for the couple to bridge this gap. All of this, of course, was unnecessary.

Aversion to your partner's body odor or the taste of their skin or private parts is going to cause avoidance and distancing. Talking about such issues can devastate the safety and security system, especially if partners are *not* secure functioning and good communicators. A great many people are sensitive to smell and touch. Some people actually have more smell sensory receptors in the olfactory parts of the brain that allow them to pick up a wider variety of smells. Some people have sensory problems with touch, including types of clothing, oils, and the like. It should also be mentioned that smell, taste, and touch are all highly influenced by memory. How we feel about certain scents and flavors is often mixed with our emotional memories when first encountering these fragrances or gustatory experiences.

I've found that many islands, in particular, suffer from problems in the near senses. Much of this can be traced to low contact maintenance in early infancy and childhood. Islands often come from island mothers who themselves have problems with contact maintenance and proximity seeking. Low-contact babies may continue as such throughout their lives, making touch problematic for them. Also, many low-touch babies or children from families where attachment values are dismissed or devalued grow up to become more sensitive to smell, taste, touch, and near vision, especially when anticipating long periods of contact maintenance. These individuals will develop an aversion to their partner through these senses and will hide or cover up these aversions with excuses. They feel shocked and ashamed by their aversive reactions and may conclude that they're not attracted to their partner. The real culprit is likely threat.

Martin and Karla, both in their early forties, became highly sexual early in their relationship. After Karla moved in with Martin, she noticed that he started physically distancing from her. She couldn't understand his actions, and he denied there was anything wrong. He'd move away from her when she approached for affection or sex. He appeared annoyed whenever she took his hand. He pulled away when she went to kiss him. Her self-esteem began to plummet as she could only surmise that he wasn't into her anymore. She eventually moved out and broke up with him.

Weeks passed before Martin begged to see her again. She agreed to meet him for dinner, and after a short meal they went back to his place and had sex. He was as engaged as ever. They continued to date throughout the next few weeks with none of the distancing experienced when they lived together.

Martin convinced Karla to give living together another try. She did, and the distancing soon returned. Karla was frustrated to no end and insisted they enter couple therapy. Martin's secret was his strong near sense aversions to Karla. He felt terrible admitting that he started to hate when she touched him, feeling trapped and unable to get away without hurting her feelings. He felt deeply embarrassed to tell her that he sometimes didn't like her breath or the sensation of her tongue in his mouth. Most difficult of all was his aversion to the smell and taste of her vagina. They were both devastated by these admissions, which were profoundly personal and embarrassing.

What Karla and Martin didn't understand was that these aversions were a manifestation of Martin's severe threat reactions to engulfment and smothering, only active when living day to day with the same lover. His aversion to Karla was like a brain fake-out. His brain and body were playing tricks on him, very believable tricks that Martin always took to mean he was with the wrong mate. Martin didn't have a history of molestation or sexual abuse. However, he recalled that this very same problem would arise in prior relationships. He had always told himself that it was a problem with the other person and not himself.

Sensory anomalies, in this case, could be due to a medical condition, and having a partner notice this would be a feature, not a bug. Medical issues must always be ruled out in the case of sudden changes in olfactory and gustatory perception of the other partner. Trust in the relationship to exist despite saying something embarrassing or something that might offend the other. Focus on the fact that your partner is telling you this to ensure intimacy continues between you, as opposed to insulting you. Avoiding matters such as these will only put the relationship in greater danger, as will taking constructive criticism as a threat. Avoidance leads to massive misinterpretations by the other partner due to lack of adequate information.

For the person experiencing aversions in the other partner, the problem could be due to just being an island, which is a mind-body issue. If so, that partner should have some memory of similar sensory experiences in past committed relationships. (Be honest about that.) In case you were wondering, people who start off having aversive sensory reactions to their partners generally don't end up living together or marrying each other. So, in the case of Martin and Karla, the sudden change in Martin's adverse sensory perceptions would more likely point to something other than a biochemical mismatch between partners. It would also be possible that Karla, who is feeling rejected by Martin and whose distress now increases before and during sex, is producing more sweat and hormonal excretions in direct response to Martin's rebuff.

Helping Martin deal with his island issues around distancing, intrusion, and enmeshment also led to calming his sense percep- tions and gradually stopping his adverse reactions to Karla's touch, smell, and taste. There are just as many women as men who have this problem.

EXERCISE
Near Senses

Just in case you thought of avoiding this matter of the near senses, I'm going to ask the two of you to talk about it together. If need be, pour yourselves a glass of wine to relax and then let's get going.

Talk frankly about your *real* experiences with smell, touch, taste, near vision (meaning up close), and sound:

- Does anything bug you in these areas?

- If so, in which senses and under what conditions?

- Did either of you ever experience problems in these sensory areas in previous relationships? If so, how did you handle it with your partner? Did you keep it to yourself? If you did, how did it change your behavior?

- How would your partner know if you had a problem with how they smell, taste, touch, look, or sound? Would you be honest? Would your partner be honest? Would you dare to ask? Would you dare to tell?

- Do you both agree to avoid talking about this altogether? If so, why? What trouble would it cause? Would it be a deal breaker?

Differences in Libido

Related to the problems with near senses are differences in libido by one or both partners. The term *libido* has many meanings. To Freud, libido refers to all instincts and drives relating to love. We commonly refer to this as sex drive. However, others have referred to libido as life energy, something that might include sexual drive but isn't limited to it. Nonetheless, sex drive is affected by gender, age, physical health, mental health, genetics, drug and alcohol use, medicines, and other psychobiological factors.

On a neurochemical level, libido is managed by the dopamine centers of the brain (such as the ventral tegmental area and the nucleus accumbens). A key player in this dopamine system is phenethylamine, which is part of that initial love potion that nature brews during the infatuation phase. Other players are testosterone, noradrenaline, estrogen, oxytocin, vasopressin, and acetylcholine.

Libido inhibitors include most antidepressant medications, beta blockers, and opioids. Libido activators include dopaminergic agents such as amphetamines and cocaine. Many physical conditions will also negatively affect libido, such as diabetes, obesity, anemia, and hypothyroidism.

Disgust

In her wonderful book *That's Disgusting: Unraveling the Mysteries of Repulsion*, psychologist Rachel Herz describes her research into this universal human emotion.[1] Others have famously covered this particular emotion, such as the naturalist Charles Darwin[2] and the psychologist Paul Ekman, whose facial action coding system identifies disgust as one of seven universal facial expressions.[3] I'm going to integrate some of their work here and take it in the direction of libidinal drives and sexual behavior.

Disgust is an emotion that comes online at around three years of age and is culturally determined and therefore learned. The brain's anterior insula is "disgust central" in that the emotion is almost entirely processed there. It's generally a revulsion to something offensive or distasteful and has its biology in response to taste, smell, sound, and vision. Certain disgusting visuals, sounds, smells, or tastes can lead to nausea and vomiting, and that reaction can be contagious. Another person vomiting serves an instinctual survival mechanism that alerts others in close proximity to poisoned water or food, thus causing a chain reaction. Many elementary school teachers know this firsthand.

This type of disgust—as a survival mechanism—is associated with life threat, such as poisoning, disease, and infection. Fears of contamination are a constant preoccupation for individuals suffering from obsessive-compulsive disorder; such individuals can experience disgust almost continuously. Fears of contamination also cross over to sociopolitical issues related to xenophobia (dislike or fear of people from other countries) and, as such, has been used by political leaders as a lever to facilitate crimes against humanity. This form of disgust leverages the fear people have of "others" bringing disease but also of those people as subhuman and therefore providing justification for genocide.

Why am I discussing the matter of disgust in a chapter about sex and libido? Because sex, pornography, body fluids, and body parts can elicit disgust in a great many people. This type of disgust is connected to superego functions related to shoulds and shouldn'ts. It's a particularly judgmental perspective that looks down upon human behaviors that are thought to be animalistic. Disgust around sex is particularly interesting because, like other forms of disgust, it's learned through familial and cultural influence. Disgust includes a typical human revulsion to the notion that humans are animals. Many people view sex as beastly, especially when engaged for purposes other than procreation. Even then, some people may find something revolting about nakedness, private parts, fluids—and even touching. This is quite apart from what I discussed above about near sense aversions, though the two are clearly related in some ways. Here we have cultural attitudes about base human desires and obscenity, behaviors that threaten our notions of what it means to be human versus animal. Where this gets interesting is in the human counterresponse to disgust, which is curiosity and flirtation with the obscene and disgusting. We rubberneck on the freeway to see the morbid scenes of a car accident. We go to frightening movies showing rape, dismemberment, and killings. We sneak a look at pornographic material and say "That's disgusting" while maintaining our gaze. We're attracted to the obscene while simultaneously demonstrating a disgust for it.

Not everyone shares that fascination and curiosity. Cultures where religion plays a strong central role in discouraging premarital sexual behaviors, and even many postmarital sexual behaviors, may inadvertently encourage secretive sexual behaviors such as chronic use of pornography. Prohibition of anything can lead to overuse and abuse of that which is prohibited. Many priests and nuns who vow celibacy are known to act out sexually. The Victorian era saw a large increase in prostitution as well as various sexual behaviors considered perverted. Similarly, during Prohibition alcohol consumption was very high.

Still, some very religious and repressive family cultures yield offspring with low sexual awareness, little or no sexual education, and little or no interpersonal stimulation.

Early Stimulation

Studies have shown that male and female individuals who masturbate have a greater understanding of how their body works. They also tend to have higher libidos compared to those who have rarely or never masturbated. One possible consideration, of course, is to start now, but masturbation alone is no panacea.

Early interpersonal stimulation, experienced as frequent and sustained face-to-face, eye-to-eye, and skin-to-skin contact with another human being, is an essential condition for social-emotional development and vitality. Allan N. Schore, one of the leading minds in the field of attachment and neuroscience, has written extensively about the experience-dependent right hemisphere in which critical periods of the infant's brain development depend on this sustained caregiver availability.[4] Lack of stimulation, as noted before, can lead to unnecessary pruning of unused brain cells and connections during the first year of life and during adolescence. This is the "use it or lose it" rule. For instance, many islands (a.k.a. avoidants) are interpersonally neglected throughout childhood and left to manage themselves. Some invent strange ways to self-stimulate and self-soothe, depending on their level of development. According to Freud, all children of a certain age are polymorphously perverse. That is to say, their sexuality goes in all directions and not according to societal norms of sexuality. The sexual developmental trajectory of many island children, because of their overreliance on autoregulation (self-stimulation and self-soothing, without the need for a person), is often outside of social norms. This adaptation isn't to be judged as it's completely natural and predictable. Island children are simply adapting to their environment. Forgive them if they have some wild sexual fantasies and masturbatory practices. They had no supervising adult with whom to interact.

Conversely, many hypersexual adults often have histories of sexual abuse, molestation, or overstimulation early in childhood. Though sexual abuse and molestation can be hyperstimulating, hypersexuality isn't necessarily caused by early abuse. A manic parent who continually overstimulates a child can lead the child to seek stimulation in all its varieties as the brain develops. What's so interesting about hypersexual individuals is that many of them lack the ability to be tender or have mature sexual relationships with adults. Sexuality for them has been confused with unmet infant needs of comfort and security. The developing brain often combines needs and desires for safety and security with other elements such as sexual drive, fear, phobia, and attachment to objects (fetishes).

Many married couples have come to me with the revelation of a fetish or bizarre sexual fantasy begging to be realized. So many of these fetishes and fantasies are clearly connected to childhood images, objects, and persons connected to attachment security needs. One clear way to see the difference between mature and immature forms of sexuality is the lack of full mutual interaction and collaboration in their partnership. Many partners will complain that their hypersexual loved one behaves in a manner that feels masturbatory, as if playing alone. They're not actually connecting in a fashion that's fully mutual and sensitive.

Other low-stimulation families yield offspring that are hyposexual. Their libidos are relatively low throughout their lifespan. We might consider some of the individuals as low arousal (see chapter 3) and as such, not as familiar with high vitality states. That doesn't mean they're depressed or low energy. It's just that their arousal set point is lower than midline. In other publications I've referred to low-arousal folks as submarines and high-arousal people as airplanes. This is an inelegant labeling of something far more complicated and nuanced, but the images of airplane and submarine seem to get the point across. Set points are pretty consistent and aren't really changeable.

Biological anthropologist Helen Fisher has provided research into this area of libido and love in general. She posits that some babies are exposed to more testosterone in utero than others and that these infants grow up with personalities that are commensurate with high testosterone. These men and women are generally high energy, aggressive, and highly sexual.[5] If correct, this might explain why some men and women maintain a very high sexual appetite into their seventies and eighties without chemical enhancement. These partners who come into my clinic are invariably high arousal (airplanes). Whether there's a confluence of arousal set points and base testosterone levels is unclear. What's clear is that these individuals are uncommon, and despite any envy one might have for their enduring libidinal energy, they too have their problems. For instance, high testosterone individuals are less likely to be monogamous and more likely to have affairs.[6] They're exciting, to be sure, but don't expect that excitement to be limited to you only.

Sue Carter, a brilliant researcher who has for years studied prairie voles and the role of oxytocin in males, has shown that males with high levels of oxytocin tend to be more relational but less sexual than other males.[7] In other words, these male prairie voles may not be hot tamales, but they're devoted to their female partners and aren't likely to stray.

Libido differences are one of the potential battle areas between partners. Partners must have honest discussions about this and other matters pertaining to sexual expectations. If there's a deal breaker lurking there somewhere, flesh it out and deal with it now! Don't brush it off. If one of you values frequent sex and sexual experimentation, now is the time to make certain the two of you are on the same page. Libido levels aren't likely to change, at least not significantly. There are many changes that can and will occur with both men and women as they age and as health problems and medications come into play. Pregnancy impacts sexual desire, as do postpartum experiences, stress levels, mood problems, hormone changes, perimenopausal and menopausal experiences, prostate issues, and many other predictable and unpredictable conditions coming down the pike.

Also, consider what's important. If your union revolves around sex, what does that mean for the safety and security system of your relationship? It would be as if you believed your partner is unworthy due to the shape of their head. Your partner can't change that.

Dos and Don'ts Regarding Sexual Frequency

- DO talk with each other about sexual drive and expectation—be honest.

- DO decide together where and how you will prioritize sexual drive in the long run.

- DO thoroughly read this chapter on sex and talk about what it means to you.

- DON'T ignore a deal breaker if one of you feels that frequent sex or sexual variety is a "must-have" feature and the other doesn't.

- DON'T assume that libido will remain the same for either or both of you.

Differences in Adventurousness, Experimentation, and Roles

Sexual experimentation is a matter of individual taste. Some couples are highly adventurous and engage in exhibitionism, fetishism, group sex, and so on. Others prefer to keep things rather traditional. As a therapist, I think I've seen and heard it all. All experimentation in the bedroom can support long-term marriage and commitment as long as both partners agree completely to what's happening and no one is hiding something from the other. If one partner is uncomfortable doing something and doesn't speak up, the other partner should be sensitive and aware enough to notice that something isn't right. Either way, this is something to not let slide and bring up down the road. Deal with it *now*. Keep in mind what I said earlier. Talk with each other about what sex means and whether the two of you are connected throughout or whether one of you feels alone and objectified. If that's the case, someone is almost always autoregulating and playing by themselves. Again, that's not sex; it's masturbation with another person.

DEEPEN YOUR LOVEMAKING

In my mind at least, the real purpose of lovemaking is to deepen your knowledge of each other, to learn about each other and to work through all your respective injuries. It should be an opportunity to become closer. If it's only about stimulation, that may become a problem. Although the regulatory function of touch is very powerful for influencing the mind and body, eye contact and vision is a powerful regulator, communicator, and stimulator.

For this reason I suggest that you make love with the lights on from time to time. Make sure that you can see each other completely and fully. See if you can maintain eye contact throughout lovemaking. You don't have to do that every time or even ever again. But try to see if it's possible. Make sure you work together by attending outward with your eyes. Inward attention will merely lead to self-consciousness or fantasy. You should see your partner's eyes as focused and present—but not staring through you. What happens when you both do this? Does eye contact make it difficult to think? Well, it should. You're disconnecting inhibitory parts of the brain that chatter, plan, predict, and overthink. These brain areas use up a lot of resources and will interfere with your body and take you out of the present moment. You would do well to stop thinking. Does it interfere with climaxing? If so, why? See if you can do it. In any case, try making eye contact even during something such as oral sex. I know that might be awkward, but there's a way to do it, at least for some of the time. Remember, love is through the eyes and it's up close. This is the time to make it personal.

Here's another thing you can try. Try saying your partner's first name while making love. Your first name is embedded deeply in amygdala memory. It's one of the first things we learn about ourselves as it's one of the first words we hear. Unfortunately it's often paired with being in trouble, especially when called from another room. Remember that if you cringe slightly when your partner calls your name loudly or sharply, it's because the amygdala also scans for threat in the environment. But your amygdala isn't just a fearmongering brain structure. It's also necessary for sensuality and lovemaking, which is why I suggest that you save your partner's first name for lovemaking and use words of endearment when calling out to your partner. Saying your partner's first name during lovemaking may be tough for you. If so, explore with your partner why it might be such. Islands definitely benefit from hearing their first name during lovemaking. One reason is that they're not accustomed to being addressed personally. Islands can often feel as if they're just tools to be used. So when addressing your partner by their first name, you're making the kind of contact (hopefully positive) that's just for them.

EXERCISE
Say My Name

You are going to take turns saying each other's first name while eye to eye (that also means up close). This is most powerful (in my opinion) when making love and using the first name with something endearing. However, you don't have to be in bed to try this exercise. You could be merely giving your partner a kiss. Try something such as "I love you, [insert name]" and, of course, say it while holding eye contact. You can change the words around so the first name comes before, in the middle, or at the end of your phrase. You can whisper, if you wish. Play with this and see what happens to you first. Did something change in you for having said your sweet nothing this way? It should have an impact on you as you're making a strong declarative to your partner. Check with your partner. What's their reaction? Keep in mind that both islands and waves may have difficulty saying and/or hearing honeyed words with the mention of their first name. Don't just listen to your partner's feedback. Watch, wait, and wonder what they'll do when you say it and just afterward (there's often a slight delay). Did what you say make them uncomfortable? Make their eyes tear up? Make their movements jerkier? Did their facial muscles begin to show controls and freeze up?

Now, do the same thing during lovemaking—during intercourse, oral sex, or whatever you're doing. See what happens. Does the first name add anything to the experience, either saying or hearing it or both?

Sex Is Important

The key throughout this and other chapters is secure functioning, which means that whatever you're doing together, you do so with full transparency, playfulness, and in a manner that's fair and sensitive. Sex is a personal and private matter between the two of you, so don't look to others as a measure for whether you're doing it right or often enough.

Playfulness should be a vital part of a couple's routine whether that be with sex, washing the dishes, bargaining for a win-win solution, or even arguing while in conflict. Playful (and humorous) couples tend to be the happiest. It's all about play, and it's been that way ever since childhood. We learn through play and we learn about ourselves and others in an atmosphere of play. Full transparency is freedom, and freedom to be yourself—to say what's eating you, to be out in the open without pretense or distortion—is nothing if not secure functioning. Transparency between you and your partner is of ground-level importance as it imbues everything you do with a sense of safety and security. Think of sex in this way: playful, exploratory, truthful, transparent, sensitive, communicative, reparative, and drained of fear, hurt, shame, and doubt. That only comes about with teamwork, with the two you committing to doing all things collaboratively and always toward curiosity and a willingness to understand and learn more about each other and yourselves.

9

HOW WELL DO YOU FIGHT?

How couples fight is just as important as how they love, and it's one of the most predictive factors for a successful relationship. All couples have conflict and will cause each other distress from time to time. There are two partners with different brains, two different personalities, many different moods and many different thought patterns: What could possibly go wrong? The answer: anything and everything. Many couples I see think that because they're in love, they should never fight. And when they do, especially when they have that first major blowup, they're concerned there's something wrong, even unrepairable, with their relationship. While this is true in some cases, more often it's because couples don't know how to communicate without inflicting harm. Since conflict and distress are the norm, it's essential that you learn to fight well and repair quickly. You're far more likely to get what you want and prevent what you don't. Arguments typically begin because you're fighting *for* something. It's possible to learn to fight well so you can handle any conflict that comes up in your relationship, both prior to and during marriage. Remember, you're a two-person psychological system, so you move in tandem as in a three-legged race—and, if not, you lose. This applies to all aspects as you live life together, including fighting.

WHY IS FIGHTING SO DIFFICULT?

The word *fighting* is crass, especially when put up against love relationships. It seems so . . . Neanderthal. We can call it something else, but the word will again be its own problem, because whatever you want to call it, conflict is usually not fun. Putting everything we've learned together so far in this book, you should know that one person's fighting is another person's "just talking." One person's yelling is another person's "being expressive."

Let's remind ourselves of the troublesome triad mentioned earlier in this book (see chapter 4). The brain's primitives, the brain's negativity bias, the predictable role of attachment insecurity, and the matter of poor coregulation between partners all play a part in why fighting is so difficult. In this chapter I'm going to provide you with lots of tools and skills for slowing down, caring for each other while in conflict, keeping your attention focused on where it should be, and tips for interactive regulation.

As a reminder, the two of you must remain orderly in your focus and your word choices. Stick to one topic and one topic only. There's no couple who can effectively manage more than one topic when under stress. We don't have enough resources for that. Keeping the topic in focus at all times without straying is highly important. Also, don't hold the stage too long. Keep conversations short and to the point. Don't make your partner sit too long. Always observe your partner for signs of stress so you can keep them within their window of tolerance. (A window of tolerance is a threshold where a person can stay engaged without feeling threatened.) Say more than you should and you risk using dangerous words or phrases that will kick up your partner's arousal. Be friendly as much as you can. Both of you should move toward mutual relief as quickly as possible and think win-win. Take care of your own fears and interests while taking care of your partner's fears and interests. Okay? I believe we're ready to start.

EXERCISE
Signal-Response

The goal of this exercise is to allow you and your partner to explore how you signal and respond to each other while talking. Start with a simple, nonconfrontational topic, something you typically don't disagree on. It can be something as minor as the weather forecast, hobbies you like, or what you plan to do tomorrow. I've provided a series of questions to help you notice if your back-and-forth is easy or strained, what it's like when your facial expressions are expressive and flat, and if you can pick up on your partner's signaling cues.

Begin by sitting across from your partner. Take a moment to relax your body, to make eye contact with your partner and to connect. Choose who will talk first and who will listen first. Let's say that partner A is the talker and partner B is the listener.

Soon after partner A starts talking, partner B should provide nonverbalized signals and responses so that partner A feels partner B's engagement. Next, discuss the following questions with each other:

- Did partner A pick up the signals?

- Was partner B attentive and responsive?

- Did partner A accurately respond to partner B's signals?

- Did partner B provide cues to partner A?

Now try something different. This time, partner A should start talking and partner B shouldn't signal or respond at all (while still facing the speaker).

- What was this experience like for partner A?

- What was this experience like for partner B?

Soon after partner A starts talking, partner B should signal nonverbally a need to talk.

- Did partner A pick up the signal?

- Did partner A respond to the signal?

- Did partner A react negatively to the signal?

- Did partner B signal clearly?

Soon after partner A starts talking, partner B nonverbally signals to demonstrate listening and understanding.

- Did partner A respond positively?

- What was partner A's experience with this?

- Did partner B signal effectively?

THE NUMBER ONE RULE IN ARGUING

Now here's the formula: you're more likely to be heard when you take care of yourself *and* your partner at the same time. Taking care of your partner includes responding accurately to your partner's signals. Take care of only yourself and you get nothing; you win nothing. Take care of only your partner and you abandon your own needs and desires.

Often, taking care of your partner is what's most difficult. You have to know how your partner thinks and feels about specific matters. You have to put yourself in their shoes before doing anything at all and prove to them verbally that you fully understand what they want, need, worry about, and are afraid of. If you don't lead with this knowledge your partner will assume that they have to do that for themselves. When that happens, not only is valuable time wasted for both of you but also your partner is already heading toward a fight-or-flight response. They will think they have to defend their interests since you obviously aren't looking out for them.

Lead with Relief

Jami and Chloe are in their early forties, and they fight a lot. It's usually over matters of fairness centered around who does what to help out the other when needed. Truth is, both can be ill-timed in their requests for help. Both wind up impinging on each other's time at work and getting angry when the intrusion is untimely or when the other partner resists and is resentful.

Jami   I keep telling you that I can't just step out of a meeting because you want me to walk your horse on my way home. You're unreasonable and unfair. It's *your* horse! I didn't want a horse. You did, and we agreed the horse would be your responsibility, not mine.

Chloe   Oh, come on, you love my horse and you know it.

Jami   That's true. I've come to love it but the fact remains . . . it's not my horse. And we agreed she'd be your responsibility.

Chloe   So you can play with her, enjoy her, and when I really need you to help me out, I'm just on my own. Is that right?

Jami   No! If I can do it on special occasions when you're in a jam, then I'm happy to do so. But you've been expecting me lately to share horse responsibilities and I say no.

Chloe   All right then, I'm on my own. We'll just do our own thing.

This is what the two women sounded like for a long time until they understood the purpose behind leading with relief. It's not about politeness; it's about biology and how to keep your audience. In the above example, Chloe and Jami lost their audiences (each other) because they squared off by ignoring the other partner's concerns. Neither did anything to relieve the other and so it escalated to war and defeat—defeat that would certainly return as hostility. No winners here.

So this is what they sounded like when they finally got the memo on leading with relief. Let's see how it goes this time.

Jami   I know you were in a jam today with the horse. It's just you and her, and you had a job interview. Sorry I couldn't respond more on the phone. I was in the middle of a staff meeting.

Chloe   I should have checked with you this morning about this interview. I just didn't think ahead.

Sorry about that. I didn't mean to interrupt your meeting. Still, I want to know that you'll be there when I absolutely need you. I realize our agreement about the horse. But there may be some times when I need you to give me a hand. I do that for you.

Jami Absolutely. Understood. I'm relieved to hear you affirm our agreement. I fear you sometimes expect me to walk and feed her when I'm working, and I would resent that.

Chloe No. I won't do that anymore. I'm just talking about emergencies I can't control.

The first rule of taking care of both you and your partner at the same time is to lead with relief. Remember those primitives you learned about in chapter 3? Well, they're more likely to run the show when you're upset. While we all know it's better to think first—to get those ambassadors engaged—before speaking or acting, in the heat of the moment the primitives are mostly running the show. So lead with relief when talking about something stressful or distressing. This will disarm your partner's primitives and assure them that you're disarmed before doing anything else. Not doing so will result in your partner remaining in suspense as to whether you're a friend or a foe. Remember, we're animals, and when threatened our brains tilt toward war. I see partners get into trouble immediately when they fail to lead with relief and instead present their view, their needs, and their fears only. That forces the other person to be on guard and think of their interests only. That's a situation that leads to squaring off and, once there, you're both in an adversarial position that's difficult to break free from.

Dos and Don'ts Regarding Leading with Relief

- DO disarm your partner's primitives immediately before explaining yourself and your motives or discussing anything else that can put your partner on the defensive.

- DO behave with friendliness when leading with relief. Be mindful of your face, vocal tone, and body movements.

- DO offer amends, accolades, appreciation, and anything that directly responds to your partner's complaint(s).

- DON'T delay when leading with relief. Anything other than an immediate, friendly, reparative response will increase your partner's threat response.

- DON'T provide your reasons, intentions, or motives. No one cares about that when they're hurt. Save that discussion for after you've fully disarmed your partner.

- DON'T pull the old "I know you are but what am I" defensive position. It won't go well for you.

When in Distress, Keep It Short and Do It Quickly

It's vital that during distress the two of you move as quickly as possible toward mutual relief. Don't dillydally. That means you both will work as fast as you can to make matters right and good for both of you, even if you have a very short amount of time. You both should work toward win-win solutions that proffer mutual relief (at least for the time being). To accomplish this relief, you have to get something done! You have to move the ball forward in some way.

I want the two of you to be really good at getting in and out of trouble quickly, at taking distressful matters off the table as swiftly as possible. That takes skill, knowledge of everything we've discussed up to this point, and a willingness to work cooperatively and collaboratively.

If the two of you remain in stress or distress for long periods, you will remember this extended sense of tension, and it will carry over to the next time. Talking (and word choice) can be a big problem when under stress or when upset. We lose the resources to think, process, and wait before reacting. Thinking, talking, parsing, and understanding words all take resources. Hit your points and turn it over to your partner. The more you talk, the more likely you will say a dangerous word or phrase. Use friendly gestures, facial expressions, and touch (if appropriate). Pare your words to the essentials and stay on point. Stick to one issue only until it's taken off the table. If you run out of time, reassure each other that the matter will be taken up again soon and that it will work out for both of you.

At the start of a conflict, remain face to face and eye to eye. We're visual animals. We receive and process crucial information when we pay attention to this region of the body. But what does this mean in terms of real life and how we relate to our partner in moments of tension? It means we need to face our partner directly. Our eyes see the world in high definition through the fovea, which is part of the macula. The fovea is the size of a pin. We're legally blind through the area outside of the fovea, meaning our vision is clearest when looking dead ahead—to the side, not so much. Because of our eyes' rapid movements, we're not aware of this limitation. For example, when we see a face at the side, such as in a glance, our amygdala is triggered due to the lack of a continuous, clear, unambiguous visual stream. If you recall, the amygdala has a major threat-sweeping function. Therefore if you're sitting to the side of your partner while in an argument, you're more likely to escalate the distress between you simply because of the mechanical limitations of the eye, the increased involvement of the amygdala, and your inability to read your partner's face from the side.

Along with this idea that we should only be face to face in moments of tension, we should also never fight by email, text, or phone. Again, because we're visual animals, vision is the most important coregulator of our nervous system. Sound comes in second. Touch can be the greatest influencer in calming us down, but it alone can also do the opposite. So . . . the eyes have it!

If you're not maintaining eye contact at close distance, you will likely fall out of real time. You will go into your head for information (memory, futurizing, obsessing) and lose the fast-moving visual stream. Without that stream you will visualize something—what do you think that will be? If you're upset with your partner, do you think you'll visualize a loving partner? No, you won't. You'll visualize a *representation* of your partner and yourself. Remember, the brain is always filling in blanks and making up stuff. If your mood is rotten, your memories will serve that state and your perceptions will distort accordingly. Just listening to each other's voice on the phone is fine when you're both feeling good, but it's not so good when you're feeling bad. Again, your visual brain will fill in the blanks and visualize whatever fits your state of mind and your mind's representation of your partner's facial expressions. I don't know about you, but I don't want to go into a fight with a disability.

YOUR VISUAL CORTEX

The occipital lobe (visual cortex) is at the very back of the brain, but there are layers that go deeper, beyond the occipital area, responsible for very complex visual integration. Perhaps the most complex visual pathway, called the ventral visual stream, travels from the occipital cortex downward through the lower temporal lobe area, passing through what's called the fusiform facial area (FFA). The FFA is required for reading faces.

Emails and texts may be great for scheduling, passing on information, and the like, but those modes of communication are trouble for partners trying to solve an interpersonal problem or coregulate distress, especially if those partners are unskilled. I've even heard of couples using emojis to communicate how they feel, and there's now research that people can take emojis or emoticons in the wrong way. The reason for this has to do with interruptions in the flow of the signal-response system.

In chapter 4 I described the signal-response system as an exquisite series of micromoments of verbal and nonverbal communication between partners that facilitate coregulation and attunement. When partners are successfully coregulating, they're making subtle corrections to the "errors" in the signal-response stream, which cause them to fall out of attunement—but only for milliseconds. They're successful because partners automatically error-correct and reattune to each other so fast that there's zero awareness of these interactive "blips." Partners will become distressed when these errors increase or sustain without correction, or if error correction fails for any reason.

Jerry is talking with Tamara, who is excited about her new job. In the middle of her talking, Jerry inserts a joke that falls flat. He sees that he disrupted Tamara's focus and attention, and immediately corrects himself by dropping any expectation of a response from her and refocuses his attention on her report to him.

Sustained misattunement—working at cross-purposes—is what leads to distress. If the couple becomes unable to reattune in a timely manner, partners may become dysregulated and spin out (toward fight or flight, or toward life threat). As you can imagine, in the case of emails and texts, there's no continuous flow of signal-response and therefore no lightning-fast way to error-correct (thus the high likelihood of sustained misattunement).

So I say with vigor, keep your eyes on the ball—which, of course, is your partner's face. When you talk, pay close attention to your partner's face and eyes; notice their shifts and changes. If something goes awry, stop the presses and find out what it is and fix it before moving forward. As I mentioned earlier, don't talk too much and don't hold the stage for too long. You're not in a monologue. Remember: two-person system. Signal-response. If you're not paying attention, you *will* fail to error-correct and you *will* misattune, which *will* lead to more errors and increasing threat. If your partner goes down, you go down. If your partner is overaroused and in fight or flight, you lose your audience and get nothing. If your partner feels trapped and can't fight or flee, they will collapse or dissociate. Same result: you lose.

Take Care of One Issue at a Time

When in conflict with each other, don't get sidetracked. Stick to one thing, and one thing only. Never move on to another topic or issue before taking the current issue off the table completely. One issue at a time. Don't try to add anything on to that one issue, for there will be trouble. It's tempting! The issue that comes up is the one that's dealt with, and nothing else until that matter is settled and both partners are relieved. Then, and only then, the other partner can perhaps bring another item to the table. So if your partner brings up a complaint about anything, your job is to take care of yourself and your partner at the same time by leading with relief and doing whatever is necessary to disarm and relieve your partner. If your partner is relieved, and signals completion, then and only then can you explain your side of it, your intentions—whatever you feel like doing, as long as it isn't undoing the relief you just created. You're both responsible for this kind of interaction. Remember, this is an arousal game. Add more to the table and you risk increasing each other's threat level, engaging your primitives without your ambassadors, and going to war. The end result? Neither of you get anything except grief.

Tensing and Relaxing

In psychobiology, we spend a lot of time studying nervous-system arousal. Arousal, in this case, focuses primarily on the autonomic nervous system. Remember, the autonomic nervous system is comprised of two tracts: sympathetic, which is energy expending; and parasympathetic, which is energy conserving. Consider one as the accelerator and the other as the brake, respectively. Our window of tolerance, you will recall, is a bandwidth of optimal arousal for remaining in social engagement and safety. The term *social engagement*, in this instance, refers to the brilliant work of the psychiatrist and scientist Stephen Porges, who developed a powerful theory on the neurobiological human experience of safety, danger, and life threat.[1] Moving out of that window into hyperarousal, we go into fight, flight, or freeze. We're experiencing danger. Moving out of windows of tolerance into hypoarousal, we go into collapse, as when experiencing a life threat where we can't fight or flee. In other words, when we're within our window of tolerance there's enough alertness and relaxation to be able to process with the whole brain. You have all oars in the water, so to speak. Outside of that window, arousal can lead to a fight-or-flight reaction, which will compromise the brain's access to sufficient oxygen and glucose needed to operate the fancy error-correcting and self-regulating structures. On the flip side, too little arousal can lead to energy conservation and withdrawal, which can cause a similar, if not worse, problem than too much arousal. Hypoarousal turns off vital brain areas that need to be on in order to process experience. Lights are off and (almost) nobody is home. Blood pressure is too low, heart rate slows too much, and alertness is compromised to a dangerous degree. This could result in stupor, stilling, or fainting.

As a coregulatory team, both partners are responsible for keeping each other within the window of tolerance. If either partner becomes hyperaroused or hypoaroused, it can be a problem. One important way for partners to achieve this balance is to use tensing and relaxing. *Tensing and relaxing, tightening and loosening,* or *holding on and letting go* are all phrases used to describe how we go into and get out of difficult moments. Think of this as you would the peristalsis of the stomach's digestive motions. When attempting to digest painful experiences, we go into the matter and get out of it, and then back into it, kind of like the ebb and flow of the ocean or the breathing pattern of in and out. When dealing with difficult subjects or situations, holding on too long increases tension and may push you or your partner out of the window of tolerance. Holding for even longer may activate your or your partner's threat system, which can bleed over to the next time you try to engage in the subject. Letting go for too long can appear as avoidance, which is dangerous as well. Anything avoided will loom larger in the minds of both partners. The only solution to overengagement and avoidance is to tense and relax.

Both of you should maintain awareness of taking too long to process or talk about anything that's stressful. Think, go in and get out, hold on and let go, tense and then relax, and drop everything so when you do come back to any stressful discussion, you'll be refreshed and ready to tackle it together.

YOU CAN BE RIGHT OR YOU CAN BE IN A RELATIONSHIP

Let's face it, we all want to be right. We want to take our opinions and needs to the grave. But believe me, there's nothing sadder than that commitment. Let's take the case of the Flying Wallendas. These are the people who for generations have done high-wire acts in the circus, across buildings, the Grand Canyon, and Niagara Falls. One of the most harrowing of their stunts was to walk a tightrope across the towers of the Condado Plaza Hotel in Puerto Rico. The long pole that they hold for their walks serves to keep them balanced. It makes sense that they would hold on to the pole no matter what, because letting it go would certainly cause them to fall.

However, on this day with tragically high winds, Karl Wallenda was blown off the wire. Because his training and steadfast belief was to hold on to the pole no matter what, he was unable to do what was necessary to save his life—drop the pole and grab the wire. People who hold on to being right can suffer a similar fate with regard to their relationships. Many a relationship is broken because somebody refused to surrender their certainty and righteousness for the relationship.

Let's review what I've said about the troublesome triad. Communication, even on a good day, is convoluted and strange. We're mostly misunderstanding each other much of the time. Memory is filled with embellishments, preservatives, emotional nuances, and just plain old made-up stuff. In other words, memory isn't reliable. It's not like the playback of a continuous video recording of an event. Perception is like a funhouse mirror, disfigured and altered by our state of mind. Given these conditions, how right can you be? Are you willing to stake your relationship on this "rightness?" If so, why would you do that? If you have a reason, you're likely oriented toward a one-person psychological system, which won't help you in creating secure attachment with your partner.

Hopefully you've come to know how perfectly imperfect human beings are and how difficult relationships can be, especially primary attachment relationships in adulthood. We're making mistakes at every moment without knowledge of having made them. Time happens way too fast for us to realize what we're doing and why. We're always going to do what's habitual, and what's habitual is based on what we've experienced. We're going to do the same things over and over again, not because we're evil but because we're automatic—plain and simple. Further, as we explored earlier, our brain has a negativity bias from birth. Without positive input we're likely to think something negative. Even more, our brain is always cutting corners and taking shortcuts. Now, how certain are you that you're right and your partner is wrong? As a couple therapist, I know for a fact that, except on very rare occasions, there are no angels and no devils. We're just people acting and reacting automatically by memory, misappraising intent, misunderstanding, and trying to remain safe and secure.

Putting the relationship first, above being right, means having to swallow one's own pride. It's painful to admit you're wrong when you've been wrong. It's even more painful to admit your *wrongs* when you've been mistreated and some part of you staunchly believes you're right. Here's an example.

Marjorie and Kent repeatedly scuffle in the car when Kent is driving too close to another car. Marjorie, known to be anxious as a passenger in cars, will start complaining when he gets too close to the car in front of him. This annoys Kent to no end. When Marjorie sees brake lights, she reflexively grabs Kent's leg, slams her right foot down as if stepping on passenger-side brakes, and lets out a "Jesus Christ!" Kent becomes startled, hits the brakes, and screams at Marjorie, who immediately screams back. He then proceeds to feign a pullover to the side of the freeway so he can threaten her with turning the car around or insisting she drive instead. This move increases her anxiety and panic, which causes her to yell louder at him. Never actually pulling over, Kent curses at Marjorie with a rant that goes on for several minutes, shouting about what a pain in the ass she is and how he hates driving anywhere with her.

If any of this sounds familiar to you, it's probably because couples have likely fought about such things since the beginning of the horse and buggy. It's the old driver-passenger predicament. Men resent being told what to do and women feel like helpless passengers who must suffer the conceit of male control.[*]

---

[*] I rarely ascribe problems according to gender, but this one, the driver-passenger issue, seems a fairly consistent complaint that I hear from men and women.

Neither Marjorie nor Kent seem amenable to apologizing to each other because each feels justifiably wronged in these instances. Yet this is an example of the hubris that prevents partners from cleaning up their messes and moving forward quickly and fluidly. Their repair attempts sound something like this:

Marjorie I'm sick and tired of you getting so close to other cars despite my begging you over and over again to please keep your distance. You do it just to get a rise out of me. It works every time, and then you blame me for reacting.

Kent Well, I'm sick and tired of you harassing me every time we get in the car. If you don't like how I drive, why don't you just drive yourself and I'll meet you . . . wherever! I don't care. But you almost got me into an accident again by startling me unnecessarily and then badgering me—endlessly badgering me. I can't take it anymore.

Ticktock, ticktock, ticktock—this goes on too long. During these back-and-forths, nothing gets accomplished, no one remembers what to do the next time, hours are ruined, the partners just get closer to death without any upside whatsoever. Here's how it *should* go:

Kent [when not driving and looking into Marjorie's eyes] I'm sorry I got so close to that car. I know you keep telling me not to and I understand it scares you. I'm an idiot for doing that. I get annoyed with your backseat driving, but there's no excuse for what I did because I know better. I'm so sorry, honey. I'm also sorry for yelling at you. I get startled when you grab my leg like that and I freak out. I know you're not doing it on purpose.

Marjorie Thank you for that. I mean it. Really. Thank you. That was sweet. I sometimes think you do this on purpose, but I know you don't. I should relax more but it's hard because I get so nervous that you'll run into the car in front of you. You know that happened to me, and I'm sensitive to that happening again. I shouldn't get so excited. I know I startled you. I'm so sorry. [She suppresses a laugh.] It's stupid, but it's a reflex. I can't really help it, honestly.

Kent I know. Okay. I'll be more considerate and not such an asshole. Okay? But it would help if you could find your way to relax a little more in the car.

Marjorie I'll try. Just . . . don't get so . . . close to the cars. I mean, think about it. If the car in front brakes really fast, you might not have time before you hit it.

Kent No, you're right. You are. Sorry, my love.

Done. Over. Onward and upward. Now, does that mean it won't happen again? No. However, if Marjorie, just before Kent starts the car, sweetly asks him to ease her nerves by paying attention to this matter, chances are high he'll do what she asks. Similarly, if Kent, just before he starts the car, gently asks Marjorie to help him feel less tense on the drive, he can also tell her he will be mindful of the cars in front of him.

The next example is my own, and it involves my daughter, Joanna. I remember a time not too long ago when I lost it with her. I was convinced that she was in the wrong and I wasn't going to apologize—no, not going to happen. She owed me an apology. Tracey told me to go fix it with her. "You're the adult, remember," said the woman who clearly didn't understand the injustice I suffered. I wasn't wrong, dammit. But I handled it badly, came down too hard, didn't listen to her; I wouldn't have it because I didn't want to hear her defense. For several moments I couldn't separate what she did from my own bad behavior. I knocked on her door and sheepishly apologized for losing my temper and yelling at her. She cried and thanked me. Then she apologized for what she did. After we both felt relieved, she explained her perception and I realized I misunderstood. As I explained my perspective, she was able to see it. As we had this "Kumbaya" moment, we deepened our relationship by admitting our blind spots and areas of injury.

Being willing to eat crow for the relationship isn't just admitting when you're wrong. It's also admitting your part in doing wrong even when feeling wronged by the other. It's being willing to take a punch without hitting back, without punishing the other, without being defensive. Tolerating the pain that comes from another person's complaint or hurt feelings is a sign of strength, not weakness.

The Art of Lowering Oneself

In the animal world, going belly up when threatened isn't the same mechanism of defense as when the animal stills and prepares to be eaten. In the first example, the animal is doing what I call "lowering oneself." Similarly, some people who study or work with dangerous animals know how to lower themselves so as not to be mistaken as predatory.[2] Humans also do this when threatened or when wanting to demonstrate friendliness. The art of lowering oneself isn't just a survival technique. It's also a skill intended to show a partner, through physicality, they intend no harm. Sometimes lowering might literally require going to the floor beneath your partner! For many, the visual of their partner physically moving to the floor, sitting cross-legged, has an immediate effect of dismantling the primitives. It's amazing to see. But lowering oneself need not always be so dramatic. It can literally be lowering your head to the side and shifting your voice or changing the expression on your face to show harmlessness. We're visual animals, so the physicality is very important. It's always fascinating to me when I see a partner who doesn't understand the art of lowering oneself to get what they want. Lowering is often incorporated into seductive behaviors or when a person is trying to persuade another with physicality and vocal tone.

The Five-Minute Argument

If you came to my clinic, at some point I would probably put you into a five-minute argument. The purpose of that would be to put you under a timed stress test to see how the two of you would do if given only five minutes. Here's the game: Choose anything that's a current hot issue in your relationship. One of you can be upset about something or want something, or perhaps it's an oldie-but-goodie that keeps on giving. The topic doesn't matter. Just choose something around which you both disagree and set a timer for five minutes. You have five minutes to get through this issue, but you must end right side up, fully relieved and prepared to move on to something else without residue. If you're unable to end right side up, then it's a fail and . . . try again. This is practice. You'll have to work collaboratively and do the things I talked about—caring for yourself and the other person at the same time, lowering yourself to appear "friendly," remaining face to face and eye to eye—in order to achieve this goal. You're not trying to cure cancer here. You don't have to resolve anything and certainly not everything. You're simply dipping your toes into sticky stuff and removing the gunk in a way that's good for both of you. That's it!

You might consider video recording yourselves. If you can, do a mock argument about something and videotape yourselves doing it. Make sure the light is good and it captures both your faces and bodies. Notice the time you waste, the things you say or do that could appear threatening to the other, the ways in which you dominate and hold the stage too long, the way your body moves or doesn't move, the way your face expresses or doesn't express, and whether you look friendly or not. Notice also your voice. Notice if you're going off topic. Notice if you're leading with relief. Also notice if you think you look like lovers or business partners.

Things to remember as your practice this exercise:

- Lead with relief.

- Make sure your partner knows precisely what you know about their wants, needs, fears, and worries. Put yourself in your partner's shoes.

- Be loving and friendly. "Lower yourself."

- Be respectful, admiring, appreciative.

- Track your partner's face, voice, and movements for signs of distress or relief.

- Tackle distress or threat without delay.

- Insist on win-win. Make it happen.

- Consider giving up the need to be absolutely right.

- Practice tensing and letting go.

I hope you have learned how important it is to lead with relief, to make eye contact when arguing, to pay attention to each other's arousal (threat) levels, and to look out for the troublesome triad, especially when dealing with hot buttons. As your relationship develops and becomes grounded in secure functioning, it will be easier to reach win-win solutions when disagreements arise.

10

WHAT DOES THE
FUTURE HOLD?

Before we end, let me speak to the matter of alternate forms of love relationships. This is obviously not a book about open marriages, polyamory, swinging, key parties, or other unconventional arrangements between adult human beings. Let it be known that I'm not a fan of alternate forms of marriage or partnership. Having said that, I live in the real world and alternate forms of partnership have been around for ages and will continue to exist. Alternative forms of partnership, such as open marriages and polyamorous arrangements, can be successful or catastrophic. I personally don't judge the choices that people make in these situations. I only care when they come to me because they're unhappy, which is almost always due to some kind of acute or chronic sense of unfairness, injustice, or insensitivity. The successful alternate partnerships don't come to see me. Many of them make their arrangements in front of me where we try to ensure that, whatever they are, their agreements are reality-based, serve both a personal and mutual good, and can be defended as such by all parties. If their arrangements pass muster, I say yay! I don't have a horse in that race. I care only about secure functioning.

Let's briefly explore the most important question facing all partners of a union, that of secure functioning. In my work as a clinician and teacher, the question always arises about secure functioning and the matter of alternate forms of "marriage." Is secure functioning restricted to two-person systems? The answer is no. But how to square this when adding more people? The answer to this question has already been stated throughout this book. Secure functioning means that all stakeholders are fully informed, on board, and engaged in preparing for what could possibly go wrong. This is accomplished by working through if/then scenarios so that everyone together can hammer out possible solutions. As with couples, transparency and honesty are going to be key. Remember, with more people comes increased complexity and conflicting interests. Enough said.

We've covered a lot of ground. You now are better informed about each other, yourselves, and the purpose of being in a committed relationship—at least from my point of view. I hope you will use this book frequently throughout your time together. Go back to do some exercises. Use it as a reference and a way to keep track of your progress. As you come to understand the principles in this book, I hope you will be more aware of other couples in your surroundings. Do you think they're secure functioning? Do they look as if they're protecting each other in public? Do you see them playing well together?

THE WORLD LOVES COUPLES

The world favors couples—always has. This has been true throughout civilized human history. There exists a tendency for persons to want to pair up others. Many of us become preoccupied with celebrity couples. Comic book fans, movie fans, and television fans "ship" (as in relationship) characters all the time. (*Shipping* is a millennial term that's slang for relationshipping, either with real or fictional characters.) Families ship family members, groups ship group members, movie studios used to ship their contract performers for publicity, and political hopefuls are sometimes shipped by their handlers. Believe it or not, all of this has been going on for a very long time. The human need to pair up others may point to a basic human need to do this to engender a feeling of hopefulness. Famed British psychoanalyst Wilfred Bion, when referring to common problems in group psychotherapy, posited that some groups, in order to avoid painful issues, will seek to pair up members.[1]

Remember the Salahis, the couple who crashed the Obama White House state dinner in 2009? They weren't invited and yet they managed to sneak in. How did they do that? Could it be that, because they were dressed up, they looked "okay?" They weren't. They were grifters, reality-show wannabes.

Though it's true that the world loves couples, it's not true that they love couples who are horrible. If partners are behaving badly, especially toward each other, people may be mesmerized for a moment, but few will want to spend time with them. Their children, by the way, usually feel the same way.

LOOK FOR MENTOR COUPLES

Be on the lookout for mentor couples—those you admire. Most often, these are couples older than the two of you. Mentor couples can serve as real-life examples of successful relationships. Authentic mentor couples aren't perfect, and it's likely their relationship trajectory wasn't without strife. On the contrary, many of the best have survived big challenges and have gained insight and wisdom through those challenges. Be sure you admire the real couple and not simply their appearance from a distance. Get to know them. Get to know how they do it. How do they handle each other when frustrated or when under stress? Ask them questions about their trials and tribulations and how they overcame them.

Of course, there's no way to know what actually goes on between two people. Nevertheless, mentor couples should have a long track record that demonstrates their authenticity. Perhaps your mentor couple will be your same age, or older, or maybe even younger. Keep a look out for them. Hang around with other couples who are happy and seem to do the things we've talked about here in this book. Keep in mind that we hang around those with whom we identify. If you hang around happy couples and those that behave in a secure-functioning manner, it will reinforce your relationship.

FUTURIZE: BECOME A MENTOR COUPLE

We need mentor couples and hopefully the two of you will become just that for others, including your friends, family, kids, and colleagues. Try futurizing your life together. Imagine your fifth anniversary. What will your relationship look like to yourselves, to others? What do you want it to look like? Imagine your tenth anniversary. What have the two of you learned? Are you a better couple? Are you proud of what you've achieved? Do others look up to you as a couple? Are you both the real deal? Are you still pointing in the same direction you were headed from the beginning? Now, travel to your twentieth anniversary (if you're young enough to have one). If you have children, what do they think about your partnership? Are you a good model for them? Do you embody secure-functioning principles that they and others can follow? Is your collaboration, friendship, and engagement with each other enviable? Is it better than what you saw with your parents? Really think about this, perhaps when you're in bed together with the lights off. Futurize, travel in time, and imagine what the relationship could be as you journey through life together. Do this instead of allowing life to just happen, with your future making itself without your direction, vision, and input. *Point* to what you want!

So many people dread doing this kind of exercise. It's not like you're preparing your eulogy or epitaph. Actually, that's not a bad idea. Let's talk a bit about death.

YOUR PARTNER COULD DIE TOMORROW

I'm not trying to be morose here. Holding in mind the possibility you could lose your partner tomorrow makes you value them today. We all tend to get into a rhythm, a zone, where we stop being fully in reality. We take things, like each other, for granted, as if nothing will change, nothing will cease to exist. That greatly affects the way we operate in the present moment. We might not want to be bothered with our partner's wants, needs, or feelings in the moment. But think about this—what would happen if you suddenly lost your partner? Shit happens. People die suddenly. Would you feel any regret? Would you wish you said or did something different? Would you want to make amends or say something heartfelt that you've been holding back? If you're unwilling to consider the cold, hard possibility that your partner may not exist tomorrow, *you're not living in reality*. Take care of business today. Spend time with your partner today. Say what needs to be said today. Fix things today. Don't put yourself in the position of having to think "I wish I did/said . . ." or "If only I could go back in time . . ." or "I should've/could've/would've . . ." You will thank me for reminding you that life passes quickly and there's no time like the present to appreciate what you have and to count your blessings.

PRACTICING GRATITUDE

While we're at it, gratitude is a key to happiness. In fact, grateful people are less likely to be depressed or unhappy. David K. Reynolds, a prolific writer and teacher of *Naikan*, a Japanese discipline that engenders feelings of gratitude, has repeatedly demonstrated the powerful antidepressant and antianxiety effects that gratefulness has on individuals.[2] Naikan posits that misery is often a result of the human inclination to focus on what's missing or what we don't have instead of taking inventory on what we're being given every day by strangers and those we love. Despite our selfishness, we're constantly being supported by others, given to by others, and, if we really took stock on a daily basis, we would realize that we could never give as much as we're getting.

EXERCISE
Naikan

Both of you do the following. Take some paper and draw three columns. At the top of column 1, write "What [partner's name] gave me." At the top of column 2, write "What I gave to [partner's name]." In the last column, write "The trouble I caused [partner's name]." It's vital that you spend at least thirty minutes on this exercise and be completely honest with yourself. You might focus on the last three months to give you a lot of data. Spend all the time you can on the first column and write down exactly what your partner gave you.

Correct examples:

- [Partner's name] made me breakfast each morning.

- [Partner's name] bought me food (be specific) from the market.

- [Partner's name] gave me a ride to work last week.

Incorrect examples:

- [Partner's name] always does good things for me.

- [Partner's name] usually rubs my back.

- [Partner's name] takes care of me.

Exhaust this list before moving on to the next column. Really meditate on this column; focus on what you got, not on the attitude of the giver. Just the facts. Next, move on to the next column and focus on specific things you gave your partner. The last column, the trouble you caused your partner, is as important as the first. There's no fourth column that asks for the trouble your partner caused you because Naikan assumes you already know that.

Correct examples:

- [Partner's name] drove me to work and I made [partner's name] late.

- I yelled at [partner's name] before going out to dinner last week.

- [Partner's name] went out of their way yesterday to pick up my medicine.

Incorrect examples:

- [Partner's name] always complains that I'm a bother.

- [Partner's name] told me that I acted badly this morning.

- I'm a terrible person and [partner's name] deserves better.

I realize this may not be your go-to exercise because it requires some work and effort. However, I promise you, if you take the time to do Naikan on each other with full honesty, you will be amazed at how the first and third columns are *always* longer than the second one. If done properly, you will likely feel moved to do or say something that expresses your thankfulness and sorrow for receiving so much despite being a pain in the ass. Try it and prove me wrong.

RESPECT AND FEAR EACH OTHER

I realize this sounds like a contradiction. I said earlier that you shouldn't fear each other. That's still true. What I mean by respect and fear each other is that you should fear losing the other through misdeeds, betrayal, or crossing a boundary on which you agreed. Strong couples are made up of strong partners willing to throw down if a boundary is crossed. If neither of you are willing to respond appropriately to a crossed line, you're screwed. You've given each other reason to lose respect.

Make no mistake, secure functioning is conditional love. Unconditional love is reserved for children and pets. You're adults. This is voluntary. Your couple bubble is only as good as your deeds demonstrate your fidelity to secure-functioning principles. Step out of line and your partner *must* lower the hammer—and vice versa. We all need to know our limits, and the two of you must hold each other to the same limits and act if those limits are violated. Remember, in effect you're saying "This is what we do, and this is what we don't do; these are our mutually agreed upon limits, not just mine."

Partners are equal stakeholders in the relationship. Together you can foster mutually assured survival and thriving or together you can foster mutually assured destruction. You're both powerful and able to opt out of this relationship if big-ticket agreements are breached without immediate repair and recompense. Fear each other out of respect for each other. Lines are drawn to protect you from each other and, moreover, to protect the safety and security of the relationship. Protect that as the foundation of your union, for without complete trust and faith in each other . . . what's the point?

RECOMMITMENT CEREMONIES

Reassess your relationship as you move forward. Consider re-upping your commitment to each other, maybe every year. Consider the idea that you can remarry each other or recommit to each other any time you want. If, for instance, your marriage ceremony was less than ideal, do it again. Why not? You can always redo things and make them better. Miss a birthday? Valentine's Day? Just do it again, even if it's not on the birthday or on Valentine's Day. It's never too late to fix things or for a do-over. It's all about error correcting, repairing, amending, making things right, and implementing grand gestures to reverse bad memories.

It might be fun to do a recommitment ceremony. You get a chance to redo vows, which—hopefully by now you know—should be mutually constructed and agreed upon. It's another way to fall in love again. Maybe we should have recommitment ceremonies built into our culture. The two of you could be part of that movement.

AND LASTLY . . .

Go easy on each other. Take care of each other. Remember that the two of you are a survival unit. Your lives as well as your happiness depend on each other as competent caregivers. It's the two of you against the world. You're the leaders, the big bosses, and the monarchs. You govern each other and everyone and everything else. Your abilities to be better people, creative, successful, good parents, good friends, and good employers hinge on you being good at each other.

ACKNOWLEDGMENTS

I would like to acknowledge my editor, Judie Harvey, for sticking with me throughout this project and encouraging me to stay on task. Also, Haven Iverson at Sounds True, for believing in me and my work, and for having a similar sensibility about secure-functioning relationships. To many of my friends over at Sounds True with whom I've worked over the years to produce this book and two audiobooks. To Tami Simon, whose brilliance and lovely mellifluous voice never cease to amaze me. To my literary agent, Emmanuelle Morgen, whose support and friendship inspire me to write. Thank you to my family, friends, students, and mentors. I am nothing without you. And finally, to all my lovely couples, who continue to delight, inspire, and surprise me with their uniqueness, loving spirit, and courageousness. I learn so much from you.

NOTES

Introduction—Why Should You "We Do"?

1. Robert Bolton and Dorothy Grover Bolton, *Listen Up or Lose Out: How to Avoid Miscommunication, Improve Relationships, and Get More Done Faster* (Nashville, TN: AMACOM, 2018), 8.
2. George E. Vaillant, *Triumphs of Experience: The Men of the Harvard Grant Study* (Cambridge, MA: Harvard University Press, 2012), 52.

Chapter 2: How Strong Is Your Couple Bubble?

1. Stan Tatkin, *Wired for Love: How Understanding Your Partner's Brain and Attachment Style Can Help You Defuse Conflict and Build a Secure Relationship* (Oakland, CA: New Harbinger, 2012), 7.
2. John Mordechai Gottman, *Marital Interaction: Experimental Investigations* (New York: Academic Press, 1979).
3. Stephen R. Covey, *How to Develop Your Family Mission Statement*, The 7 Habits Family Leadership Series, read by the author (Salt Lake City: FranklinCovey on Brilliance Audio, 2012), CD.

Chapter 3: Managing Your Negative Brain

1. Carl Jung, *The Red Book: Liber Novus*, ed. and trans. Sonu Shamdasani, trans. Mark Kyburz and John Peck (New York: W. W. Norton, 2009).
2. Rick Hanson and Richard Mendius, *Buddha's Brain: The Practical Neuroscience of Happiness, Love, and Wisdom* (Oakland, CA: New Harbinger Publications, 2009).

Chapter 4: The Troublesome Triad: Memory, Perception, and Communication

1. Edward Z. Tronick, "Things Still to Be Done on the Still-Face Effect," *Infancy* 4, no. 4 (2003): 475–82; Lauren B. Adamson and Janet E. Frick, "The Still Face: A History of a Shared Experimental Paradigm," *Infancy* 4, no. 4 (2003): 451–73.

Chapter 5: What Are Your Styles of Relating?

1. John Bowlby, *Loss: Sadness and Depression,* Attachment and Loss, vol. 3 (New York: Basic Books, 1980).
2. Inge Bretherton, "The Roots and Growing Points of Attachment Theory," in *Attachment Across the Life Cycle*, eds. Colin Murray Parkes, Joan Stevenson-Hinde, and Peter Marris (Abingdon, UK: Routledge, 1991), 9–32.
3. Harry Frederick Harlow and Clara Mears, *The Human Model: Primate Perspectives* (London: V. H. Winston, 1979).
4. Stan Tatkin, "Allergic to Hope: Angry Resistant Attachment and a One-Person Psychology Within a Two-Person Psychological System," *Psychotherapy in Australia* 18, no. 1 (2011): 66–73.
5. Mary Main, Erik Hesse, and Ruth Goldwyn, "Studying Differences in Language Usage in Recounting Attachment History: An Introduction to the AAI," in *Clinical Applications of the Adult Attachment Interview*, eds. Howard Steele and Miriam Steele (New York: Guilford Press, 2008), 31–68.
6. Mary Main and Erik Hesse, "Parents' Unresolved Traumatic Experiences Are Related to Infant Disorganized Attachment Status: Is Frightened and/or Frightening Parent Behavior the Linking Mechanism?" in *Attachment During the Preschool Years: Theory, Research, and Intervention*, eds. Mark T. Greenberg, Dante Cicchetti, and E. Mark Cummings (Chicago: University of Chicago Press, 1990), 161–82; Allan N. Schore, *Affect Dysregulation and Disorders of the Self* (New York: W. W. Norton, 2003).

Chapter 6: How Well Do You Know Each Other?

1. Harville Hendrix, "The Evolution of Imago Relationship Therapy: A Personal and Professional Journey," *Journal of Imago Relationship Therapy* 1, no. 1 (1996): 1–17.
2. John M. Gottman, *The Marriage Clinic: A Scientifically Based Marital Therapy* (New York: W. W. Norton, 1999); Margaret S. Mahler, *The Selected Papers of Margaret S. Mahler, Volume II: Separation-Individuation* (New York: Jason Aronson, 1979).

Chapter 7: Deal Breakers

1. Ellyn Bader, Peter T. Pearson, and Judith D. Schwartz, *Tell Me No Lies* (New York: St. Martin's Press, 2001).

Chapter 8: Sex!

1. Rachel Herz, *That's Disgusting: Unraveling the Mysteries of Repulsion* (New York: W. W. Norton, 2012).
2. Charles Darwin, *The Expression of the Emotions in Man and Animals*, 2nd ed., ed. Francis Darwin (Cambridge, UK: Cambridge University Press, 2009).
3. Paul Ekman and Erika L. Rosenberg, eds., *What the Face Reveals: Basic and Applied Studies of Spontaneous Expression Using the Facial Action Coding System (FACS)*, 2nd ed., Series in Affective Science (New York: Oxford University Press, 2005).
4. Allan N. Schore, *Affect Regulation and the Origin of the Self: The Neurobiology of Emotional Development* (Hillsdale, NJ: Lawrence Erlbaum Associates, 1994).
5. Helen Fisher, *Why Him? Why Her? Finding Real Love by Understanding Your Personality Type* (New York: Henry Holt, 2009).
6. Sari M. van Anders and Katherine L. Goldey, "Testosterone and Partnering Are Linked via Relationship Status for Women and 'Relationship Orientation' for Men," *Hormones and Behavior* 58, no. 5 (November 2010): 820–26.

7. C. Sue Carter, Angela J. Grippo, Hossein Pournajafi-Nazarloo, Michael G. Ruscio, and Stephen W. Porges, "Oxytocin, Vasopressin, and Sociality," *Progress in Brain Research* 170 (2008): 331–36.

Chapter 9: How Well Do You Fight?

1. Stephen W. Porges, "The Polyvagal Theory: Phylogenetic Substrates of a Social Nervous System," *International Journal of Psychophysiology* 42, no. 2 (2001): 123–46.
2. Laura Rose La Barge, "Predator Recognition Behaviors and Stress Hormones in an Endangered Captive Mammal: Implications for Reintroduction" (honors thesis, SUNY College of Environmental Science and Forestry, 2015), digitalcommons.esf.edu/cgi/viewcontent.cgi?article=1072&context=honors.

Chapter 10: What Does the Future Hold?

1. Wilfred Bion, "Experiences in Groups: III," *Human Relations* 2, no. 1 (1949): 13–22.
2. David K. Reynolds, *Naikan Psychotherapy: Meditation for Self-Development* (Chicago: University of Chicago Press, 1983).

ABOUT THE AUTHOR

Stan Tatkin, PsyD, MFT, is a clinician, teacher, and developer of a Psychobiological Approach to Couple Therapy® (PACT). He has a clinical practice in Calabasas, California, and is cofounder of the PACT Institute for training other mental health professionals to use this method in their clinical practice both domestically and abroad.

In addition, Dr. Tatkin teaches and supervises family medicine residents at Kaiser Permanente, Woodland Hills, California, and is an assistant clinical professor at the UCLA David Geffen School of Medicine, Department of Family Medicine. Dr. Tatkin is on the board of directors of Lifespan Learning Institute and serves as a founding member on Relationships First Counsel, a nonprofit organization founded by Harville Hendrix and Helen LaKelly Hunt.

He is the author of *Wired for Dating, Wired for Love, Your Brain on Love, Relationship RX,* and coauthor of *Love and War in Intimate Relationships.*

ABOUT SOUNDS TRUE

Sounds True is a multimedia publisher whose mission is to inspire and support personal transformation and spiritual awakening. Founded in 1985 and located in Boulder, Colorado, we work with many of the leading spiritual teachers, thinkers, healers, and visionary artists of our time. We strive with every title to preserve the essential "living wisdom" of the author or artist. It is our goal to create products that not only provide information to a reader or listener, but that also embody the quality of a wisdom transmission.

For those seeking genuine transformation, Sounds True is your trusted partner. At SoundsTrue.com you will find a wealth of free resources to support your journey, including exclusive weekly audio interviews, free downloads, interactive learning tools, and other special savings on all our titles.

To learn more, please visit SoundsTrue.com/freegifts or call us toll-free at 800.333.9185.

SOUNDS TRUE
many voices, one journey